RIDING QUICKBOOKS TO THE PROMISED LAND

Need a QuickBooks Checkup?

Wondering if you have your QuickBooks system set up correctly? Have a nagging question that you just can't seem to find the answer to? Maybe you're looking to create Lists or Reports to help you get the most out of QuickBooks?

Whatever you're looking for, Jason Osser CPA & Associates offers complimentary QuickBooks Checkups to qualifying firms that will help unveil these mysteries. Areas we will evaluate include the following:

1. Bank and Credit Card Accounts
2. Assets and Accumulated Depreciation
3. Accounts Receivable Aging Summary tied to General Ledger
4. Interest and principle on loan payments
5. Year-end adjusting entries recorded

To find out if you qualify and to schedule your free QuickBooks Checkup, visit:

www.QuickBooksCheckups.com

RIDING QUICKBOOKS TO THE PROMISED LAND

How the World's Most Successful Entrepreneurs
Use the World's Most Popular Accounting Software
To Make More Money in Less Time

JASON OSSER CPA MBA

POWER HOUSE PUBLISHING

ALEXANDRIA
VIRGINIA

Riding QuickBooks to The Promised Land

How the world's most successful entrepreneurs use the world's most popular accounting software to make more money in less time

by Jason Osser

Published by:
Powerhouse Publishing
625 N. Washington Street, Suite 425
Alexandria, Virginia 22314
info@powerhousepublishing.net
703-982-0984

Copyright ©2018 Jason Osser

All rights reserved. No part of this book may be reproduced in any form or by any means electronic or mechanical including but not limited to photocopying, recording, or by any information storage and retrieval system without written permission from the authors except for the inclusion of brief quotations in a review.

ISBN First Paperback Edition: 1986179265

First paperback printing March 2018
Printed in the United States of America

Osser, Jason
Riding QuickBooks to the promised land, how the world's most successful entrepreneurs use the world's most popular accounting software to make more money in less time

1st paperback ed.

ISBN-10: 1986179265
ISBN-13: 978-1986179263

Library of Congress Control Number: 2018946114

Cover photo of Jason Osser by Mike Olliver. Motorcycle courtesy Bull Run Harley-Davidson. Background photo by Mark Basarab (Unsplash).

What Business Owners Are Saying About This Book

I run a small business in Virginia and QuickBooks has always given me a great deal of stress. This is the best book I've read on QuickBooks, and I really feel that I now have a clear understanding of how to set things up and get the reports I need to make business decisions quickly. I also found the chapter on Retirement Planning for Business Owners very helpful. Thank you, Mr. Osser!

Martin Saenz, Co-Founder
Lighted Signs Direct

In simple terms, Jason explained how using QuickBooks properly can make your business a success. This book will help your business get where you want it to go; it makes accounting and QuickBooks, part of the success of your business routine by making them understandable, important, and automatic. Just like turning on the lights.

Mauricio J. Tamargo, Attorney at Law
Poblete Tamargo LLP

As a real estate investor both in and out of a self-directed IRA, I have found Jason and his teachings to be a wealth of knowledge. This book gives the clearest direction I have ever seen of how to leverage QuickBooks as a tool to maximize your profits – which is the reason most people chose entrepreneurship in the first place!

Forrest Odend'hal
Real Estate Broker

Dedication

I dedicate this book to my loving and supportive wife Yiping, and our beautiful daughters, Alexandria and Jessica. Yiping has encouraged my business ventures over the years and spent untold hours helping me proofread this book. My love and gratitude also go to Alexandria, who created and drew the cartoon in front of this book, and to Jessica who shares my unique sense of humor.

Acknowledgements

A number of people were instrumental in helping me write this book. First, I want to acknowledge my friend and client Martin Saenz for persuading me that I could help a lot of people by sharing what I know about QuickBooks, and that writing this book was the best way to do that. Next, I want to thank Frank Felker of Powerhouse Publishing for his guidance and support throughout this process. Finally, I take my hat off to Chris Taylor, General Manager, and all the good folks at Bull Run Harley-Davidson, for hosting the photo shoot for our cover and my book launch party. You guys rock!

About the Author

Jason Osser graduated from State University of New York at Oneonta with a Bachelor of Science in Accounting and Economics, and from Binghamton University with a Master of Business Administration with a concentration in Human Resource Management.

After relocating to the Washington, DC metropolitan area in 1996, Jason held a series accounting positions, from staff accountant to controller, until he decided to own and run his own business. Since leaving corporate America nearly 15 years ago, Jason has been a successful franchise business owner, an accounting and small business expert, a Certified Public Accountant, a real estate investor, and an adjunct professor at local colleges. Jason's diverse experience enables him to bring insights into how to create a growing and successful small business through disciplined accounting best practices and tax planning.

Although real estate investing started out as a personal hobby, Jason has since expanded that investment portfolio and shared his knowledge and experience with others along the way. Particularly, Jason is the spokesperson for Long and Foster Real

Estate, giving seminars and presentations on how to invest in real estate using Self-Directed IRAs.

To stay current with the latest rules, regulations, and tax law changes, Jason frequently attends conferences and seminars, and pays for his staff to do the same. In addition to teaching classes and seminars to give back to the community, Jason has been a member of the Greater Springfield Chamber of Commerce for over 10 years. He has also served both as treasurer and board member of Stop Child Abuse Now (SCAN).

Jason Osser can be reached by telephone at 571-331-1652, by email at jso@ossercpa.com and on the web at http://www.ossercpa.com.

Disclaimer

This book has been published for informational purposes only. You should seek the advice of a qualified professional to assist you with your accounting and tax needs. Although the author, Jason Osser, and the publisher, Powerhouse Publishing, have made every effort to ensure that the information in this book was correct at the time of publication, neither Jason Osser nor Powerhouse Publishing assume, and hereby disclaim, any liability to any party for any loss, damage, or disruption caused by errors or omissions, whether such errors or omissions result from negligence, accident, or any other cause.

Neither Jason Osser nor Powerhouse Publishing are affiliated with Intuit Software, makers of QuickBooks. Intuit has not endorsed this book nor Jason Osser's training videos.

Table of Contents

Foreword 23

Chapter 1   Accounting 101 25

Chapter 2   Your Business Entity 39

Chapter 3   Which Version of QuickBooks is Right for You? . . 49

Chapter 4   Setting Up QuickBooks the Right Way 63

Chapter 5   Creating and Using Lists 79

Chapter 6   Managing Payables and Receivables 89

Chapter 7   Reporting & Budgeting 99

Chapter 8   Working with Inventory 111

Chapter 9   Your Business and Your Taxes 117

Chapter 10 Retirement Planning for Business Owners . . 139

Foreword

As a long-time client and friend of Jason Osser, I am extremely excited about the publication of this book. In my experience, no one knows about QuickBooks, and how small business owners can use it to their advantage, as well as Jason does.

As an entrepreneur and real estate investor, I keep a lot of accounting records. Many of my investments have complicated ledger entries involving depreciation and interest calculations, which must all be entered correctly into QuickBooks, so my reports give me the information I need to run my businesses profitably.

I enjoy working with Jason because of his responsiveness, knowledge, and entrepreneurial experience. He is much more than your typical accountant. He owned several businesses before becoming a CPA and combines real life experience with his accounting and tax education and knowledge.

Over the past 8 years, my business has steadily grown, and Jason's been an integral part of making that happen. In addition to handling my bookkeeping, accounting, budgeting, tax preparation and planning, he is also my CFO and trusted advisor. His experience in Human Resources has also been invaluable to me on more than one occasion.

Jason has a gift for taking complicated subject matter and making it easier to understand, which is exactly what he has done with this book. Like me, you are fortunate to have Jason Osser come into your life and business. Trust what he tells you in this book and call him if you need further guidance. That's what I did 8 years ago, and it was one of the best business decisions I've ever made.

Elizabeth Lucchesi
Team Leader, Liz Luke Team
Long & Foster Real Estate

Chapter 1

Accounting 101

To get the most out of QuickBooks, you need to have at least a general understanding of how accounting works. As an owner of multiple businesses, I want to share with you the knowledge and experience I have accumulated that have benefited my businesses, to give you some insight into what you'll be entering into QuickBooks, and why.

In this chapter, I am going to cover the following:

- "No, You Can't Just Use Your Checkbook."
- Balance Sheet
- Assets
- Liabilities
- Equity
- Income Statement
- Revenue
- Expenses
- Cost of Goods Sold
- Cash vs Accrual Accounting
- Double Entry Accounting – Debits and Credits

"No, You Can't Just Use Your Checkbook"

Every year I meet new clients who have attempted to manage their accounting using a checkbook. Sometimes they're smiling, but more often they're crying. And the reason is that, at the end of the year, when it comes time to file their taxes and report income and expenses, they don't know how the business did, because the checkbook can't tell them that. Why not?

Several years ago, I met with a new client in the roofing business. It was our first meeting, so he wanted me to know his biggest concern. "My bank statement says that I have a lot of money, but QuickBooks says that I am overdrawn by $500,000! Even so, I think I'm doing okay, because I have a lot of money in the bank."Clearly, this business owner was not in control of his accounting.

I found two problems immediately. His bank statement and his QuickBooks account were so far out of alignment, because he hadn't reconciled them in months. And the reason he had so much money in the bank was that he hadn't been paying his vendors – and they were beginning to send collection letters. This story illustrates just one reason why managing your accounting via your checkbook is a very bad idea.

Here is another simple example. Say your business has a vehicle and you took out a loan on that vehicle. Your monthly payment on the loan is $500, which consists of principal and interest. Now let's assume that, for this month, $50 of your payment was for interest and the other $450 was to reduce your principal. Only the interest of $50 may affect your profitability. How could all this be represented in a checkbook? Well, not very easily, and probably not at all.

There are also expenses for items such as meals, that you can't fully deduct. You may be purchasing inventory, which will reduce the balance in your bank account as you pay for it, but it will not affect your profitability until that inventory is sold. At that point, it becomes an expense known as Cost of Goods Sold.

The reason you're in business is because you want to do well and be successful. To do that, you need to understand how your business is doing. QuickBooks is a scorecard that gives you that understanding. To use the scorecard, you need to follow the rules to have a fair evaluation and a fair measure of your business performance.

For the remainder of this chapter, I will describe the key accounting terms you need to understand.

Balance Sheet

First, we'll look at the balance sheet, which is a snapshot of your business's net worth at any given time. The balance sheet report is one of the two most frequently used financial statements. For some clients, I run this report monthly. But, for most, I do it for at the end of the year, so we can determine the value of the business. The balance sheet consists of assets, liabilities, and owners' equity at a particular point in time.

Assets

On a conceptual level, an asset is something your business or your company owns that is going to bring value or is going to make you money.

Some examples of assets include:

- Bank Accounts – this is the cash you have now.
- Account Receivables – if someone owes money to your business, that is money you will soon have.
- Inventory – inventory is something that you have that you intend to resell. You will mark it up and make a profit on it.
- Business Vehicles –if you have a vehicle owned by your business, the purpose is to use it so that you can make money.

Other types of assets include anything you use to make money for your business, even if you don't think about these things as assets. For example, I am an accountant and I do tax preparation and accounting work for my clients. For that, I need a computer. I also need a desk and a chair. If I don't have a desk or a chair, it's going to be really hard for me to do my work. Those are all normal assets of my business. These are things that are going to help me generate a profit and help me make money.

Liabilities

The second part of the balance sheet is liabilities. Liabilities are essentially the opposite of assets. If assets are the things to help you make money, liabilities are what you owe to others.

Common forms of liabilities are loans or credit card balances. You may have a truck loan or an equipment loan. You may have a line of credit, or you may have one or more credit cards that you use in your business. I have credit cards. I love them, and I pay mine in full every month. But until that end of the month comes, every time I buy office supplies or something else, I'm increasing the amount of a liability that I owe the credit card company. That liability doesn't go away until I cut them a check.

Equity

Equity is the result of taking all of your assets, which is everything that you own, and subtracting all of your liabilities, which is everything that you owe to other people. Whatever is left over is the good stuff; that's your equity. Equity is what shows the value of your business.

Here is a simple example: if you have $20,000 cash in the bank (asset) and $5,000 on your business loan (liability) that leaves you $15,000 when you subtract the liability from the asset. That is what your business is worth. That's what the equity account measures.

Say you're running your report on December 31st. If you reconcile your bank accounts, which we'll get into in a later chapter, then the money in the bank accounts is going to correctly show on the balance sheet as an asset. And you'll know what the loan balances are, because those will be tied to loan schedules from the bank. Then you'll be able to see what is left. That's your equity, and that's the value of your company.

Income Statement

As mentioned before, the balance sheet is one of the two most common financial statements; the other is the income statement.

The two main accounts on the income statement are revenue and expenses.

Revenue

If you are in the lawn-cutting business, your revenue is the money you make from cutting lawns. If you own an ice cream shop, your revenue is money you make from selling sundaes and ice cream cones. That's where your income comes from.

One of the great things about accounting is we get to customize how we categorize revenue based on our business need. Most businesses that I work with, typically have one to three revenue accounts, which are usually different types of services. For example, in my business, I want to see how much money I made doing tax returns, so that might be one revenue account. I also do a lot of general accounting throughout the year for different clients, so that would be another revenue account.

That is information just for me, as the business owner, because I find it valuable to know how much money I make in revenue in one area of the business versus another. As far as the IRS is concerned, assuming your primary business is where all that money is coming from, it all goes to the same place and that is one tax line called "gross receipts" or "sales," which is your revenue.

Expenses

Expenses, by definition, are any payments you make which are ordinary and necessary for your business.

To determine what qualifies, you would look at similar businesses to see what a normal expense is for that type of business. People often ask if they can write off things that aren't really business expenses. For example, someone owns a flower shop and they bring their dog Fluffy to work every day, because they love her, and she doesn't like being alone. But they can't leave the shop to walk her, so they hire a dog walker. And they ask if fees they pay the dog walker can be considered a deductible business expense. My answer is no, that is a personal expense, which is not ordinary or necessary for operating the flower shop.

Now, let's examine a second example of the flower shop. This flower shop is in a really bad part of town, and there's a history of robberies and problems at night. The owner has a trained guard dog at the flower shop, and its job is to bark and scare everyone away, so they are less likely to rob the shop. Well, in that case, we could probably determine that the dog is an ordinary and necessary expense for the shop, because there is a business purpose for that dog to be there. Therefore, we could deduct normal, necessary food, walking, or expenses that may be involved with that dog.

Expenses get pretty interesting. As you are setting up expense accounts for your business, you need to ask yourself: "Can I justify this as ordinary and necessary for my operation?" A lot of times it is confusing, and you want to seek guidance of a CPA to help you better understand what can be treated as valid business expense.

Cost of Goods Sold

Cost Of Goods Sold (COGS) is a big expense for many businesses. COGS is the cost of selling your product, usually material supplies and labor. It is an expense, but it's a separate category of expense, because we like to know what the costs are involved in the direct sale of our product. For the example of an ice cream shop, the cost of goods sold is going to be the ice cream, the cones, and the employees who scoop the ice cream.

Cash versus Accrual Accounting

The next thing you need to understand is the difference between cash-based and accrual-based accounting. They are basically two different ways of deciding when you recognize that a sale has been made and/or an expense has been incurred. The timing could impact how much profit you report in a given time period.

Let's say you're selling ice cream and you're using cash-based accounting. In cash-based accounting, if in one month you took in $8,000 selling ice cream cones and sundaes, that's your revenue for the month. Next, let's look at your expenses. During that month you wrote checks to pay rent, electricity, and so on. Only the checks you wrote during that month would be counted toward expenses using cash-based accounting. And when you subtract the expenses you paid during the month from the revenue you took in during the month, your profit will be the difference.

Let's say you are in the food catering business, and it's the holiday season. You just got a big order for Christmas Eve — you're going to cater a party with 100 people for a $5,000 fee. On December 24th, you do a wonderful job catering the party, they thank you, and you give them the invoice before you leave. January 10th of the following year, you open your mailbox to find the check for $5,000.

Question: when does that $5,000 become revenue? Do you record it on December 24th when you did the work, or do you record it on January 10th of the following year when you got paid for it?

Answer: It depends, it depends on whether you are a cash basis taxpayer or accrual basis taxpayer.

If you elected to be an accrual basis taxpayer, you are going to record that $5,000 in revenue on December 24th. If you are a cash basis taxpayer, you would not record that as revenue until the work was completed and you received the money. In this case, you didn't receive the money until January of the following year, so you would record the income in January.

Let's think about this for a second. If you're a small business owner and you have to pay taxes on this money, would you prefer to pay taxes included as money in December when you don't have the money yet? Because, when we do your tax return, if you elect accrual basis, that's counted as part of your income, and you're going to pay taxes on it in a few months, when you file your return. If you are on a cash basis, then you have another whole year before you have to pay taxes on that money.

For that reason, a lot of businesses, from a tax standpoint, prefer the cash basis.

Now, with expenses, it's very similar. If you're on an accrual basis, you have to record expenses when they were incurred. For example, let's say that it's December and you had the electricity running in the ice cream shop, and you were making ice cream cakes and other treats. You don't get your electricity bill until January, but they're actually billing you in January for what you used in December.

Well, on the accrual basis, you would have to make some entries to account for this, because that was really a December expense, even though you didn't get the bill until January. However, on the cash basis, you don't record it as an expense until you pay the bill. So, that would be an expense of the following year.

In a later chapter, I'll go into how to run financial analysis reports in QuickBooks. You'll see that at the top of the report, you'll be able to change between the cash basis and the accrual basis, and you can see the differences by running the report both ways.

Double Entry Accounting – Debits and Credits

The final bit of basic accounting you need to know is double entry accounting. Yes, we're going to be talking a bit about debits and credits, but there's no need to panic.

I'm going to spend just a little bit of time on this to give you an overview, but there is a lot to it. Basically, it is a system of checks and balances. It's kind of like in science, where there is positive energy and there is negative energy. It's the same general type of concept in accounting. It's Yin and Yang.

Whenever you do any type of activity, it causes two things to happen in the world of accounting. The activity could be something as simple as the computer mouse broke and you need to buy a new one.

You go down to the local store and buy a new mouse. Two accounting entries happen when you do that. One entry is the expense. You bought a mouse, so there will be an entry called "mouse" under expenses. It's a $20 office supply. The other entry that happened is you paid cash, so the cash went down $20. Every entry you make, there are actually two sides to that entry to help keep it in check.

That's what the double entry system of accounting means. The counter-balancing entries are called debits and credits.

If you have the time, and this is something you want to learn more about, I advise taking an introductory accounting course in addition to reading this book. A course in basic accounting will provide a much stronger foundation for what we're doing.

For more information, visit our video library:
http://www.OsserCPA.com/videos

Chapter 2

Your Business Entity

Choosing the correct form of business entity is a major decision small business owners face. It is helpful to have your business entity selected before you begin working with QuickBooks so that you can set everything up properly when you begin. In this chapter, I will discuss factors to consider when selecting what entity is best suited for your business.

- Six impacting factors:
  - Ease of Setup
  - Limited Liability
  - Tax Consequences
  - Capitalization
  - Management
  - Owner Transition/Sale of Business
- Common types of entities:
  - Sole Proprietorship
  - Partnership
  - Limited Liability Company (LLC)
  - S Corporation
  - C Corporation

"What type of entity is a best fit for my business" is usually one of the first questions people ask me. My response to this question is always: "It depends." There is not a definitive answer, because each person's business needs are unique.

What type of business are you in? Is this a start-up or an existing business? What are the risks associated with your business? How many people own the business? Do you have employees? What is your household income? These are the few questions I normally ask my clients to help them determine how they should set up their businesses.

A Realtor and Her Business

I work with over 100 small business owners on an ongoing basis. One who comes to mind relative to this chapter is a successful real estate agent whose business I have seen grow and change over the years. When she first came to me she was operating as a sole proprietor. After I explained some of the liabilities she would be personally responsible for if something went terribly wrong with a real estate transaction, she agreed to move to a single-member LLC (Limited Liability Company). As her business continued to grow, it later made sense for her to become an S Corporation. With the recent changes created in the 2018 tax law, we may consider changing her business form again.

As you can see, there are a lot of options here and what makes sense for you can change over time.

Let's take a look at the factors you need to consider when selecting the correct form of entity for your business.

Six Impacting Factors

1. Ease of Setup

A sole proprietorship is the easiest of all the entities to set up. Just by starting a business, if you chose nothing else, your default entity is sole proprietor. If you're a 15-year-old kid, spending the summer cutting your neighbor's lawns, assuming you file the correct paperwork with your local governing agency, you are a sole proprietor. Other entities such as an LLC, S Corporation, or a C Corporation require more time, expense, and paperwork to create.

2. Limited Liability

One consideration for choosing the right entity type for your business is the level of personal liability you are willing to undertake. For instance, if something goes wrong (we're a litigious society) and you get sued, what are you liable for personally? For certain entities, the liability is limited to the business's assets, meaning that you can't personally lose more than the value of your business. Whereas with other entities, such as the sole proprietor, unlimited personal liability is one of the downsides. Not only your business can be at risk, so can your personal assets.

3. Tax Consequences

Many business owners look for ways to reduce their income tax liabilities. Selecting the appropriate entity may have substantial tax implications for your business. This is one of my specialty areas of accounting, and I have devoted all of Chapter 9 to a discussion of taxes, tax law changes, and ways to maximize tax benefits.

4. Capitalization

The next area that we look at is how your entity choice affects the capitalization of the business. How are you going to inject the startup money every business needs to launch? For a lot of smaller businesses, that may not be a big concern. If you're going to start a lawn mowing business, you buy a used lawnmower for $100 and get started. But what if you're starting a major software company or a big restaurant that costs millions of dollars to build and to staff? Suddenly, capitalization becomes a very important consideration. How do we get the money in? Are we selling stock? Are we borrowing money to finance the business? More complex capitalization methods require more sophisticated entity setups.

5. Management

A question for slightly larger businesses is how the management is going to work? If you're a sole proprietor, you're the chief, the cook, and the bottle washer. If you're starting a larger company, it's very possible that you will bring in a team of managers, and you may create a board of directors to oversee the business operation. Will you need to offer them stock options in order to attract a high level of talent? If so, you need to create a type of business that can accommodate that.

6. Owner Transition/Sale of the Business

People start businesses for many different reasons, but they frequently don't think about how they would like to exit their business. The end game might be that they want to retire in 20 years, and they want to have enough money to retire comfortably. That's great. But when the time comes, how do they successfully transition out of the business?

For a sole proprietor, it works like this. You're Joe, and you start Joe's Lawn Mowing Service as a sole proprietorship. When the day comes that you decide to stop mowing lawns, you close the shop, and your business ends. But at a Fortune 500 company, like Coca-Cola, if the president retires tomorrow, it doesn't really affect the company. Coca-Cola will bring in a new president and the company will go on about its business.

Common Types of Entities

Sole Proprietorship

With a sole proprietorship, there is no separate business entity, which means both you and your business are one and the same. Business owners frequently choose this entity type, because it's the easiest to set up and the associated costs are minimal. Special tax benefits that come under the 2018 tax reform that are applicable to sole proprietorships are discussed in detail in Chapter 9 of this book.

Partnerships

A partnership is really very similar to a sole proprietorship, except that it consists of more than one person. Years ago, in the 1970s and earlier, partnerships were very common. But they have become less popular in recent years, because many businesses prefer the LLC structure that offers limited liability to the owners.

Limited Liability Company (LLC)

One major advantage to setting up your business as an LLC is liability protection. If you have the lawn mowing company and, God forbid, you damage a customer's property, or you hurt someone, your company may be sued. If that company is an LLC, your liability is limited to the value of your company. As a sole proprietor or general partner, your personal assets can be at risk.

A question to ask when starting an LLC is how many people are going to own the business? If there is only one person in the LLC, it's called a Single Member LLC. As a Single Member LLC, the tax filings are identical to a sole proprietor. If your LLC has more than one owner, it will be classified as a Multi-Member LLC, which will file a separate tax return, usually on Form 1065. More details on this are described in Chapter 9.

The best protection you can get, no matter what types of business entity you have is a great insurance policy. At a minimum, you should purchase liability insurance. Depending on your profession, there may be other insurance policies, such as errors and omissions, that you should also consider purchasing. In addition, I recommend that you buy an umbrella policy that will give you additional coverage fairly inexpensively.

S Corporation

If you elect to be an S Corporation, you must first either establish your business as an LLC or a C Corporation, and then you can further elect to be taxed as an S Corporation.

Over the past 20 or so years, many LLCs and some C Corporations made the election to be taxed as an S corporation. There are several reasons for doing so including that S Corporations are not required to pay FICA tax on the profits of the business, which could lead to a tax savings of up to 15.3%. In 2018, Congress will be discussing ways to help fund the new 2018 tax law, which is expected to increase the capital debt by $1.5 trillion over the next 10 years. One way that Congress in looking to fund this shortfall is by reducing entitlement programs. Congress is considering making the profits from S corporations subject to FICA tax.

Another complication with S corporations is that small business owners with pass-through income may be entitled to a credit of up to 20% on their Qualified Business Income (QBI). The profits of a business may qualify for this 20% credit, but the salary that you would pay yourself as the owner of an S Corporation is not entitled to that 20% credit.

Let's look at an example. Say that you own Joe's Lawn Mowing Service Inc., and you are an S Corporation. As the owner of the S Corporation you must pay yourself a fair and reasonable salary. You decide that $60,000 for the year qualifies as fair and reasonable and your S Corporation makes a profit of $40,000. In this example, you would be entitled to a 20% reduction on the profits of the business, and you would only have to pay federal income tax on the $32,000 profit from your business and your $60,000 salary for a total of $92,000 of federal income.

Now let's say that instead of being an S Corporation, you decide to be an LLC. In this example, you would not receive any W-2 income from your business, so your business would show income of $100,000, of which you would be entitled to a 20% credit and you would have $80,000 of federal income.

S Corporations also have additional expenses related to payroll processing. With the changes in the 2018 tax law, you should speak with a CPA to determine if an S Corporation is still a good choice for your business.

C Corporation

Unlike a partnership, an LLC, or an S Corporation, which are pass-through entities (meaning that the income taxes are paid on individual owner's tax returns), a C Corporation pays its own taxes. In other words, the C Corporation itself is actually going to be paying taxes on the profits that it makes, which leads to a lot more tax planning for small business C Corporations. The 2018 tax reform has reduced the tax rate of C Corporations to 21% and has repealed the Alternative Minimum Tax (AMT) on all C Corporations, making this a more attractive option for some firms. Again, I have discussed this subject in detail in Chapter 9.

For more information, visit our video library: http://www.OsserCPA.com/videos

Chapter 3

Which Version of QuickBooks is Right for You?

There are several versions of QuickBooks, and my clients often ask which version is the right one for them. My answer is that it will depend on your business. I'll describe the options in more detail below but, in general, I most often recommend the desktop version. The reason is simply that, from a cost perspective over a multi-year period, the desktop version of QuickBooks is the least expensive option; it is the easiest to operate, AND it has the most bells and whistles.

In this chapter, I will discuss:

- Desktop Versions, Online Versions, Macintosh
- Pro, Premier and Enterprise
- Subscription Plans
- Licenses and Upgrades
- Switching Between Versions and Plans
- QuickBooks Payroll
- QuickBooks POS (Point Of Sale system)

The Chef Who Ran His Books On His Phone

I recently gave a seminar on How to Use QuickBooks for Your Business to an audience of professional chefs. After my presentation, one chef approached me to say that his version of QuickBooks couldn't perform many of the tasks I had just described. He handed me his phone where I found that he was using a version called QuickBooks for the Self-Employed, which is available for a discounted price of $5.00 per month.

The old adage that "You get what you pay for" certainly applied here. Not only would his version not perform most of the functions I teach or recommend, we're also having a hard time transferring his data into the correct version of QuickBooks for his company's needs. For a one-time cost of about $200, he could have purchased the desktop version of QuickBooks Pro, which would work perfectly for three years. That works out to $5.55 per month. Take a moment to read this chapter and determine which version best fits your needs and your business.

The Big Picture

Here is a high-level overview of the desktop and online versions. If you want to know details about what is available in each version, I recommend looking at the QuickBooks comparison chart online at https://quickbooks.intuit.com/products/. The features change with every update, so the most current information will be available on the website.

QuickBooks Versions: Desktop and Online

Desktop

As the name suggests, the desktop version is designed for use on a desktop computer at one location, such as a shop or an office. There are three major versions of QuickBooks for desktop; Pro, Premier, and Enterprise. I will discuss each of these in detail later in the chapter.

QuickBooks desktop is an amazing product. Starting at around $200 for the Pro version, you get approximately three years of use out of a program that can serve the accounting needs of most small business. That's a great value.

Be forewarned that you may need to upgrade your computer to effectively run the QuickBooks Desktop versions. QuickBooks for desktop has a ton of capabilities, and that means the software crunches a lot of data and uses a lot of memory. This is particularly true as Intuit keeps advancing those capabilities with each new version. Therefore, you want to have a fairly new computer to effectively run the software.

I tell my clients if their computer is more than two years old, particularly if it's a less expensive computer, to look at the computer's hardware and RAM compared to the requirements listed on the software box. When in doubt, upgrade your computer. Powerful new PCs are very inexpensive these days and your one-time investment here will pay dividends for years to come in the form of time savings and reporting power. After all, making more money in less time is what QuickBooks – and this book – are all about.

Online

The biggest advantage of the online version is the ability to easily access your QuickBooks data from any location. It is also good if you have different types of computers or devices which will be accessing the same information. For example, with the online version you could use tablets, iPads, laptops, or even smart phones to access your data.

Most often, my clients use the online version if they work remotely or have custom or industry-specific software they use. For example, my clients include law firms, veterinary clinics, and other businesses that use a separate billing system customized to their industry. QuickBooks online versions can frequently integrate with these other platforms.

Macintosh

I mention the Mac version here primarily to note that, while Intuit did previously sell a Mac version, it was discontinued a few years ago. You may still be able to purchase it, but support from Intuit may be limited. For the Mac community, the online version is the best option.

Best of Both Worlds

For business owners who want the best of both worlds — the functionality of the desktop version with the ease of accessing the program remotely online — there are services that host your desktop in the cloud. That means you can run the desktop version of QuickBooks Pro, Premier, or Enterprise in the cloud.

This option will add an extra monthly fee of $50 or more, depending on the service and number of users. However, if you are, for example, a high-commission salesperson where time is of the essence and you want a reliable data capture and reporting solution with the flexibility of remote access, it's a great option. There are many good cloud server providers on the market. I have personally used Swizznet and found that they do a great job hosting the different QuickBooks versions.

QuickBooks Desktop Pro, Premier, and Enterprise

If you choose QuickBooks desktop, you have three versions to choose from: Pro, Premier, and Enterprise.

QuickBooks Pro is the version I use with the vast majority of my clients, because it does a very good job of capturing the items most small businesses need. From a cost and functionality standpoint, it is a great value. You can purchase it for around $200 (per user, with a maximum of three users). Intuit does yearly updates, so if you enjoy the latest bells and whistles you can update it every year (more on that later). However, most of my clients keep it for about three years, because QuickBooks tends to support the current year they're selling for a three-year period. When they stop supporting it, I strongly encourage upgrading to the newest version.

QuickBooks Premier is around $350 (per user, with a maximum of five users). Premier makes sense for certain industries, such as construction, because it has some additional industry-specific reports that are extremely helpful. In fact, some industry-specific functionalities are only available when you upgrade to Premier or Enterprise.

Finally, QuickBooks Enterprise costs around $1,100 for one user. If you have a fairly big, established company, Enterprise is the version you need. With Enterprise, you can have up to 30 users.

Accountant's Copy

All of the desktop versions have a feature called accountant's copy, which lets you separate part of the year's data so your accountant can work on it without disrupting your daily operations. For example, it's January and you need help from your accountant cleaning up your records for the end of last year, so you can get your taxes ready. But your store is still open for business and you need to use your QuickBooks in January to ring in sales and track revenue.

Accountant's Copy allows you to choose a cut-off date, say December 31. You can then send your accountant a copy of your file, and the accountant can change the data, reconcile, and fix things up until the December 31 date. Meanwhile, you can keep using QuickBooks for your daily accounting January 1 and forward. Your accountant can work on the file as long as necessary and it won't impact you at all. When he's done, he'll email that program back to you and you incorporate the changes into your QuickBooks. And, just like that, your QuickBooks is up to date for last year.

Accountant's Copy is a wonderful feature I use often with my clients. The downside is there is an extra step, because you're emailing files back and forth and putting in cut-off dates, as opposed to the online version where everything happens live. But, even with that extra step, we find that, from a time and efficiency standpoint, we are able to get work done a little more quickly with the desktop version.

Licenses

All three desktop versions can be set up so that you may have multiple people working on QuickBooks simultaneously. The Pro version only allows you to have up to three people on it concurrently. So, if you have a slightly larger number of staff and you need more than three people using the program at the same time, you would normally go to the

Premier version, which allows up to five concurrent users. For large companies, Enterprise allows 30 simultaneous users.

Upgrades

If you're thinking of upgrading, this is what I tell my clients to consider: October is when Intuit releases the newest version of QuickBooks. By newest version, I mean QuickBooks has its "model year," so to speak. The program released in October of 2017 was QuickBooks 2018. That program should last you for three years. After three years of service from a given model year, I encourage you to upgrade because Intuit's support is going to stop.

So, if you were to buy QuickBooks 2018, and a year later QuickBooks 2019 comes out with a new feature you think will be very beneficial to your company, you may decide to upgrade. In that case, you would pay the full purchase price to upgrade to 2019.

QuickBooks Online

Currently there are four online versions available, with prices ranging from $10 to $50 per month. They are called Self-Employed, Simple Start, Essentials, and Plus.

The Self-Employed version (which was mentioned in the Chef story at the beginning of this chapter) is extremely basic and has very limited functionality. It does not have double-entry accounting. I have recently had issues with some clients incorrectly selecting this version for their business and being stuck with a version that was too limited for them to effectively use. The data that is entered into this product cannot be exported to a more advanced version of QuickBooks.

The Simple Start version is *very* basic. For business owners with a few employees and yearly sales ranging from $100,000 to a few millions, the basic online version is extremely limited and does not do standard tasks that I would like for the business to have.

The Essentials is a vast improvement compared to the aforementioned versions. However, it is still lacking in functionality such as inventory tracking, budgeting, management of 1099s, and etc. For just a few dollars more a month, you can upgrade to the Plus online version.

Most of my clients who use QuickBooks online use the Plus version, which runs about $50 a month. Even though that is the price, Intuit frequently offers substantial discounts to encourage people to subscribe.

One of the benefits of QuickBooks online is that you can access it anywhere. For example, you could give your accountant a way to access your account where they don't need any special permission. They can fix your data in real time and help you with your accounting needs remotely.

Another benefit of the online version is the integration with other software tools. This may prove necessary for particular types of businesses that uses specialized systems for billing or receivables. Having said that, it is helpful to evaluate integration needs or speak to a CPA to determine the value that the online version can add to your business.

One of the biggest shortcomings of the online version is that it has been around a relatively short period of time compared to the desktop version. It has been developed almost as a separate product, so it does not have the same functionality and it is not as user-friendly.

Subscription Plans

Intuit, like many other software companies, offers a monthly subscription for its online QuickBooks program. For the latest on pricing and system functionality, be sure the visit the Intuit website.

Switching to a Different Version

You are able to switch from one version to another (with the exception of the Self-Employed online version); either from desktop to online or the other way around. I've had quite a few clients who have moved from online to the desktop version, when they see how much easier the desktop version is to use. They are even happier, when they realize the cost savings, too.

Payroll and POS Systems

The basic QuickBooks versions handle your accounting functions. QuickBooks also offers add-on products not everyone needs. The two most common are payroll and a POS (point of sale) system.

Payroll

If you have employees, you must pay them through payroll. If your business is set up as any type of corporation, either an S-Corp or a C-Corp, and you, as an owner of the company, work in the business, then you will also be on payroll.

So now the question is, how do you do payroll? I prefer working with businesses that specialize in payroll such as ADP or PayChex. There are also some good local providers in many communities.

QuickBooks offers a "do-it-yourself" or a "full-service" option to process your payroll. The "do-it-yourself" option allows you to add a payroll module to the version (desktop or online) of your QuickBooks product. You will process the payroll on your own and be responsible for tax filings associated with it. The "full-service" option is similar to having a third-party payroll provider where Intuit will process and submit payroll on your behalf.

I am not a big fan of the do-it-yourself QuickBooks payroll offering. This is because payroll is a fairly complex procedure where you are dealing with multiple taxing agencies. As the owner of the company you are responsible for making sure that all taxes are remitted on time and correctly to the correct taxing agency. I have personally observed too many small business owners spend too much time dealing with payroll tax issues. I prefer to use a full-service provider whose responsibility is to remit your taxes and file your forms on time for you.

POS System

Point Of Sale (POS) Systems are for businesses that have inventory and need a way to track that inventory to properly sell their products. Your POS system should keep track of your inventory and be able to determine your cost of goods sold. Most POS systems use bar codes which you are able to scan into the computer.

Your POS system appears to just be recording a sale, but the system is actually performing multiple calculations in the background. Let's say you have a retail store and you sell a bag of dog food. You would scan the dog food and have your customer pay you for the food. Here is what the POS is doing behind the scenes:

1. Your POS system is subtracting one bag of dog food from your inventory and keeping track of how much you have left. Your POS system should have the ability to alert you that you

may have to order more bags of dog food when your inventory level falls below the threshold that you set.

2. The POS system takes the cost of what you paid for that bag and reduces your inventory total by that amount. So if you had $10,000 in inventory and sold one bag of dog food with a cost of goods sold of $10, the system would reduce your inventory value to $9,990.

3. The POS system will create an expense called Cost of Goods sold for the $10 that you paid for the dog food.

4. If you sold this bag of dog food for $20, then the POS system would record that your revenue and cash both increased by $20

QuickBooks offers a POS product as an add-on. There are also several good third-party POS systems on the market that integrate with QuickBooks.

For more information, visit our video library:
http://www.OsserCPA.com/videos

Chapter 4

Setting Up QuickBooks the Right Way

By now, you know which version of QuickBooks is right for you, and you have nailed down the form of your business entity such as a sole proprietorship, partnership or LLC. In this chapter, I'm going discuss the setup options in QuickBooks, including:

- Basic Business Information
- Your Industry
- Company Organization
- What You Sell
- How You Sell
- Sales Tax
- Creating Estimates
- Start Date
- Chart of Accounts
- Customers, Jobs and Vendors
- Bank Accounts and Credit Cards
- Lists
- Inventory Items
- Historical Transactions

Constructing The Chart of Accounts

I have a wonderful client who is in the home construction and remodeling business. They had installed, set up and been using QuickBooks for three years, before I became their accountant. When I first looked at their data, I saw a lot of things that didn't make sense. They had accounts I had never heard of. They had liabilities listed as assets and expenses listed as liabilities – it was just all over the place.

I asked them, "How did all this happen? Who set QuickBooks up for you?" They told me that they had set it up themselves and just did the best they could at the time, assuming everything would get straightened out at some point. "You've filed your past two years' tax returns based on this?" I asked. "Yes," they answered, "is there a problem?"

I tell you this story to emphasize how important it is to set QuickBooks up correctly in the beginning, so it can do its best work for you going forward. We were able to get their situation straightened out, but not without a good deal of expense and hassle.

The great thing is that QuickBooks is user friendly and customizable, so the setup is simple. However, you do need to do it right from the start; this chapter explains what the options are and why they're important, so you can set them up correctly for you and your business.

A Quick Overview of the Setup Process

As soon you open your program, you're going to have a series of tasks to complete and questions to answer. You will find a handful of required fields and you won't be able to go to the next screen until you complete them. This is general information, such as your company name, business address, etc.

Once you get beyond those required fields, everything else can be done later if you need to gather information. I mention that because some people get nervous if they happen to be missing a small piece of information. I suggest setting up as much as you can immediately, and then go back later if anything is missing.

Here are the steps in the order that QuickBooks has you fill them out. This following paragraphs also give you a preview of the information you need to gather for each step.

Note: I based this list off the QuickBooks Pro desktop version because that's what most of my clients use. These items should be available on the other desktop versions and some online versions as well. However, if the online versions do not have every function, we go through on this list, and you realize you need it, you can usually upgrade.

Enter Your Business Information

The general information required for the initial setup includes your company name, address, phone number, fax, business email, website, and EIN or Social Security Number. It is important that this fundamental information is correct because it will appear on many forms and statements including your invoices, reports, and tax forms.

Choose Your Industry

The next thing is choosing your industry, which is one of the nice features of QuickBooks that makes the rest of your setup easier. Remember the flower shop with the dog we discussed in an earlier chapter? The owner isn't sure what types of items are ordinary and necessary expenses. Fortunately, QuickBooks knows that certain industries have certain types of income and expense accounts, or balance sheet accounts. The industry list includes about 40 major industries. If you see your industry there, select it, and QuickBooks does a great job of automatically setting up an initial Chart of Accounts. We'll later explain what the Chart of Accounts is and how you may modify it as needed.

Don't see your industry on the list. No problem. At the very end of the list of all the industries, QuickBooks has a general services option and a general product sales option. If you're in a service-based business, you can choose the general services account and customize the generic Chart of Accounts later to fit your needs. Same with a products-based company where you have inventory or sell merchandise.

Company Organization

Knowing what type of entity your business is impacts how your Chart of Accounts is set up. When QuickBooks sets up your Chart of Accounts, it's going to set up your equity account slightly differently depending on the type of organization you are. For example, let's say you're a sole proprietor, QuickBooks will set up the equity account with you as the owner. Now, let's say you're a partnership, QuickBooks will then know that there are at least two people, so it's going to set up multiple owners of the equity account.

Setting up the company organization correctly in QuickBooks makes using the program easier, and QuickBooks offers flexibility for you to change this setup later when necessary. For instance, if you are a sole proprietor, but later convert your entity to a partnership, you can go back and update your equity accounts to include additional partners.

The correct setup of your company organization will affect the tax mapping in QuickBooks. In other words, QuickBooks knows, based on the type of entity you are, which tax forms your data flows to. Is it flowing to a Schedule C 1040? Is it flowing to Form 1065? An 1120? Or an 1120-S? If you choose to use the tax mapping function, the information will integrate with some tax software programs. I usually don't use the tax mapping feature, because I find it easier to do the tax returns manually, rather than setting up the mapping.

What You Sell

The next thing QuickBooks is going to ask you is what you sell. There are a few things that go into answering this. Most companies sell services, products, or both. For example, I'm in a service-based business. I do tax returns and accounting. I don't sell products.

This is important because, most of the time, service-related industries do not have to charge sales tax. QuickBooks knows that if you're just selling a service, you don't have to set up the sales tax module because you're not charging sales tax. Also, because I'm selling a service, I don't have an inventory module.

What if you sell products and have inventory? Well, then you need those things. By checking that you have product, you're telling QuickBooks that you're going to need to look at sales tax, and will need to set up an inventory account to track inventory.

QuickBooks knows what you need and sets up those parts of the program correctly, so you don't have to. You can just pop on the screen and say, "Oh, there's inventory. It's already set up for me. I can easily add my inventory items."

How You Sell

Select whether you'll be using invoices and/or sales orders. If you are not sure, here is an overview of each of these forms.

Invoices

Most of my clients use the invoicing function, and it's a great tool that tracks a whole lot of information. Let's say you hired me to do your taxes. I'm going to invoice you for that. I'm going to enter all of your information like your name, address, and the cost and services I performed. I can create an invoice in less than a minute and send it to you, because all the information is in one place.

Then QuickBooks records who owes me money in an Accounts Receivable Report. Until you pay me, the report shows you still owe me. Then, when you pay me, I can apply the payment against the invoice and have a record that you did pay me. It's a very clean and easy way to track your invoices and be sure that people are paying you on time.

Sales Orders

The next most common sales tool is the sales order. Again, QuickBooks sales orders are based on your needs. Sales orders are good for things like the jelly you sell at a farmer's market. You're not as concerned with who bought jelly. You don't really need to know that, because they already paid with cash for it, and you may or may not see that person again. You're not trying to stay in contact with that person, other than you hope they come back to the market and buy from you another time. All you really want to capture is how much jelly you sold and how much you made. Everyone who bought jelly paid you cash, so you can enter one sales order at the end of the day. You can call it Item Q, which stands for quick sale. You can put in your sales for the day or the week, just to track that information. You know that you sold $2,000 worth of jelly and put $2,000 in the bank.

Sales orders can work like an old tape register. If you have a little calculator and a little tin box that you're taking money in, you could run a tape where, at the end of the day, it will show you how many sales you did. You can just look at that and do one entry for everyone.

Tracking sales is where QuickBooks Point of Sale integration could come into play. If you sell inventory and you have a storefront, you are going to need some type of POS system to track it. There are many POS products on the market that integrate with QuickBooks, including one made by QuickBooks.

Sales Tax Information

Depending on where you distribute your products or services, and how many places you may pay sales tax to, QuickBooks will help you set up multiple sales tax accounts. For example, let's say you do farmer's markets on the weekends, and you sell your jelly in two or three different states, you would have to report sales tax in the states and the jurisdictions in those states. QuickBooks will let you track multiple tax agencies very easily. At the end of your reporting period, you'll be able to run reports and pay each of those jurisdictions based on the sales taxes you owe them.

Creating Estimates

QuickBooks allows you to create an estimated price for a project for a client without it being an invoice. If the client moves ahead and purchases that product or service, you can convert that estimate into an invoice.

To do this, you choose the option to use estimates. Let's say you're in construction, catering, or any type of business where the client expects a detailed estimate of what's involved in the project. You can create detailed estimates, and modify them as needed.

Say a client is remodeling their kitchen and you give them an estimate. Then they think about it and they say, "We still want this, this, this, but this other thing, we don't want anymore." You can easily modify the estimate and add or delete whatever you need to give them the new estimate. Then they say, "Perfect. That's what we want," and you can convert the updated estimate into an invoice once the work has been completed.

Choose a Start Date

Choosing a start date for your business is important and I strongly suggest you speak to your CPA about this. The purpose of a start date is to record when your business entity started. If it started on June 27, we could enter that as a start date. The more important question is when you do your taxes, what is your tax year going to be?

The vast majority of small businesses that I work with are on a calendar-based tax year, which runs January 1 to December 31. But you may have reasons to have a different calendar year. We still want to bring that into our analysis of what the start date is going to be. I generally prefer a start date of January 1 for most of my clients, even if they started later in the year, simply because it makes some of the reporting a little bit easier.

One of the things you have to track, particularly for new business starting out, is if you incurred expenses before your business started. Those expenses are called start-up costs. You want to work with a CPA to help you with this, because you need to identify those expenses separately from your regular costs. My rule of thumb is, generally, enter the first of the year as the start date, but understand there may be reasons not to.

Review the Chart of Accounts

Now it's time to review the Chart of Accounts that QuickBooks generated based upon the industry you selected earlier in this process. These pre-populated accounts are based on what most people in that industry use, and include assets, liabilities, equity, revenue, and expense accounts.

QuickBooks gives you a fairly long list of recommendations, and on that list, it's going to pre-select the ones it thinks are the most common and most beneficial to you (by putting a check next to each). Now you're going to go down that list and check additional accounts that are recommended but maybe not included in the checklist, because they aren't as common, or you can uncheck some that you know you don't need for your business.

That is going to create a basic Chart of Accounts, which makes things easier for you. You'll still be able to go back in at a later time and add, adjust, or remove specific accounts as you need to.

Setting up Customers/Jobs and Vendors

The next thing on our checklist is entering your customers and your vendors.

If you are a brand new business, QuickBooks gives you an option to enter your Customers, Jobs and Vendors in the start-up phase. Normally I would enter things as they're happening. For example, if this is your first time paying a new vendor, when you go into the pay bills section, you'll set up that vendor to pay them for the first time.

The same process is true for invoices. You'll have the opportunity to add all the customer information or add all the customer detail when you create an invoice.

If you have maintained a long list of clients or vendors, you may choose to import the list instead of manually entering each one in QuickBooks. By following the import file format QuickBooks sets up, you can easily complete the data import process, saving you both time and money.

Setting up Bank and Credit Card Accounts

With any type of business, no matter what type of entity you are, I always recommend you use separate bank accounts and separate credit cards from your personal accounts. You create the accounts as if your business just opened today, and you put your first money in the bank account as your opening equity to start the business.

Let's say you open today and you put $5,000 in your business bank account to start it. I would normally enter that $5,000 in the opening sheet and enter the date it was put in. Then QuickBooks will make the journal entry to show that you deposited $5,000, and you have $5,000 of equity. If you're a more established business, then you should really speak to your CPA again to be sure the accounts are set up correctly.

You can also enter a historical amount, if you had the account before you set up QuickBooks. If you're going to enter a historical amount, I usually want it the last day of the previous year. For example, if we're on a January 1 through December 31 tax year, which most of you will probably be on, and you started using QuickBooks in 2018, I would pre-enter the balance of the bank account as of December 31, 2017.

Similarly, with credit cards, you may need to see prior transactions and enter them in QuickBooks. This is particularly true if you don't pay off your credit card in full every month.

Lists Items

Now let's talk about lists. QuickBooks has three main ways of entering information. One is a register that is kind of like an old checkbook register where you record information. If you go to the register screen, it actually looks like an older paper checkbook. The second way of entering data is through forms, such as an invoice or a bill that you're paying.

The third way of entering data into QuickBooks is through lists. The purpose of a list is to make it easy for you to enter repetitive information. For example, let's say that I sell a lot of strawberry jelly. Every time I sell it to a client, I don't want to have to type in a quantity, a description, a price, and everything else for that jelly. I can enter it one time in a list and I can record all that information. Then, the next time I sell that jelly, I can type in an abbreviation that I set up, and the description will carry forward and the prices will carry forward.

There are three types of lists you need to know about. They're called one-sided, two-sided, and three-sided, which has to do with how we set it up as an item list.

One of the first questions QuickBooks is going to ask you is what type of item list you want, and it will give you a list of six to ten things to choose from.

To understand a one-sided transaction, just from a conceptual standpoint, let's look at the tax return I did for you. That is one thing I did. I could set up a list called Tax Returns and pre-fill in a description. I could also pre-fill in a price and that way, when I type in "tax," all that information will appear.

For a two-sided transaction, let's say my accounting firm does the accounting for your business and one of my employees does the work. On the same two-sided transaction, I will record both the rate for which I pay my employee and the rate at which I bill my client.

Three-side transactions are normally inventory related. Let's go back to my jelly business. First let's assume I purchase the jelly somewhere else and I mark it up. The very first item in the transaction is I'm purchasing the jelly, and it's going to become inventory until I sell it. I hold on to it for a little bit, then next week I go to a farmer's market and sell the jelly.

At the point I sell the jelly, two things happen. The jelly is no longer in inventory. It left inventory and it now becomes a cost of goods sold, because I can now recognize that as an expense. Then the third thing that happened is I made money, because I sold that jelly to a customer so I have revenue.

In this example, there are actually three sides to this transaction – firstly I receive the inventory, secondly the inventory is converted to cost of goods sold when a sale is made, and lastly, we recognize the revenue from the sale.

Inventory Items

One thing to note: there is a slight difference with inventory evaluation based on which version of QuickBooks you purchase. I'm not going to get into a lot of detail, but you should speak to your CPA about this if you have questions, because they are set up differently.

The desktop version of QuickBooks, for inventory, uses an average inventory valuation method while the online QuickBooks uses a FIFO (first in, first out) method. I mention this because you need to know that for tax purposes. And, if you are in a business that uses inventory and you ever switch from one version of QuickBooks to another, you want to be aware that your inventory valuation will change, and some adjustments would need to be made.

Historical Transactions

The last item to discuss here is historical information. Most of the setup is designed for someone who has a new business or is new to QuickBooks. But let's say you've been in business for multiple years and this is the first year that you made the plunge to QuickBooks. You want to be sure that you're doing the setup correctly. One of the factors is how much historical information we want to enter and what the value of that information is.

For example, let's say you have some clients that owe you money and you have written it down in an Excel spreadsheet or somewhere else. You know who they are and how much they owe you. You may choose to enter the amount owed in a lump sum for each client, or enter each invoice for a detailed breakdown. When it comes to credit cards, if you're not paying your credit card bills in full every month, you may have to enter previous credit card information.

For more information, visit our video library:
http://www.OsserCPA.com/videos

Chapter 5

Creating and Using Lists

Congratulations, you've set up QuickBooks! Now it's time to dive into some of the cool features it offers, starting with lists. Lists will quickly become your best friends, because they make the functionality of QuickBooks more consistent and a whole lot easier.

In this chapter I'm going to cover:

- What Lists Are and Why You Want to Use Them
- The Chart of Accounts
- Setting up Customer Lists
- Setting up Vendor Lists
- The Employee Center
- The Lead Center
- Importing Data into Lists

What Lists Are and Why You Want to Use Them

Here's a great example of the power of using Lists within QuickBooks. I had a client who owned a landscaping company. They were spending hours and hours every month, inputting client invoices for simple services like mowing lawns. I showed them how to create lists containing customers' information and common services they provide. Now they just start typing and QuickBooks does the rest, filling in addresses, pricing, everything. They now save almost a full day of invoicing every month, and it only took a few hours to set up the lists.

Three Ways to Enter Information into QuickBooks; Forms, Registers, and Lists.

Forms

In a form, you are manually filling-in every piece of information, from customer name to item description to pricing. There are times when this is the best approach, such as when you are entering a first-time transaction. But, repeatedly entering data which never changes from entry to entry becomes tiresome and inefficient.

Registers

Using a register in QuickBooks is just like using a checkbook register. I usually don't use register to capture data because they only collect very basic information. But if you are most comfortable with something that works like a paper checkbook register, you can certainly use it.

Lists

The advantage of using a list is that it simplifies entering items with repetitive information. When you use a list, the repetitive information is entered exactly the same way every time. You'll always know that, if you're invoicing a certain client for example, the billing information and terms will always be the same.

Here is an example of why a list is useful. You're selling items in your furniture store and you have different types of inventory. In a list, you can put in a description of each item. Then, every time you enter that item, you know what price you're selling it for, the cost from the vendor, and what the invoice description should be. If a customer buys a 6-foot maple hutch, you can select that from a list and know that all the data surrounding that transaction will be correct. The consistency of the list helps you track inventory.

Selecting the correct item from a list is easy too. When you type in a couple of letters for an item code, the list will display one or more items that match. You choose the one you want, and it will populate all the data in QuickBooks.

Now that you know why lists are helpful, let's talk about the types of lists you will use in QuickBooks.

Chart of Accounts & Item Lists

The Holy Grail of all lists, at least to an accountant, is the Chart of Accounts. It is a list of all the accounts you have for your business: assets, liabilities, equity, revenue, and expenses. This is where your accountant will go to see the overall health of your business.

The Chart of Accounts is a list that you can adjust over time. If you have a new expense category, you can easily add that to the Chart of Accounts. Or if you need to rename or delete something, you can also do that. Accountants also like Item lists. Common items in this list include - inventory, different types of revenue, and sales tax that you may need to remit. In my opinion, item lists are sometimes underutilized and, if set up and used correctly, can save your business time and money.

Setting Up Customer Lists

QuickBooks gives you the opportunity to capture customer information and then use it repetitively going forward via lists. Customer lists help you keep track of all the information associated with your customer account: point of contact for billing, terms, jobs, estimates, and so on.

There are a couple of ways to set up customer lists. The first is to go to the customer center and create a new customer. QuickBooks will take you through a customer setup, where you enter all the critical information that you want from a customer: name, address, phone number, email, website address, etc.

Sometimes, though, you may not want to go through the customer center. Let's say you're creating an invoice and the customer name isn't already in the system. QuickBooks is going to recognize that, and from within the invoice, it's automatically going to put you into the customer center to enter that new customer.

Once you're in the customer center setting up a new customer, you will see several different tabs. The customer name is really all QuickBooks requires, but often you're going to want more information. For example, you want their address so you can mail them an invoice if needed. You're going to want a phone number and email address so you can contact them. You're going to need to know if, for example, they pay sales tax.

Following is a list of a few useful tabs.

Jobs Tab

The Jobs Tab lets you assign different jobs to that customer. One of the industries, for instance the construction industry, frequently uses the "Jobs" tab for keeping track of different projects.

Here's an example of creating a job under that tab. You're doing a bathroom and kitchen remodel on the Smith's house. You can set up jobs as a sub-account to that customer, so you know you're doing two different projects for the same customer, a bathroom and a kitchen in this case. Then, on the Jobs Tab, you can keep track of where each project is: Do you just have an estimate or have you started work yet? Or, is the project completed? You can use that tab to monitor the process.

Additional Information Tab

This is where you can assign different sales reps to different customers. I find that, for businesses that either pay on commission or want to track how a sales rep is doing in relation to the financial reports, this is an extremely useful function. This allows us to run profit and losses and other financial statements for any sales reps in your company.

Payment Settings Tab:

Through Payment Settings, QuickBooks manages two types of information. Firstly, it records payment terms. For example, some businesses might give a small discount if customers pay within a certain amount of time. One frequently used discount is called 2/10 net 30, which means that, if the customer pays within 10 days, they'll get a 2% discount off the bill. If they don't do that, the full amount is due within 30 days. You can set up these payment terms under this tab, along with a credit limit.

Secondly, you can put credit card information in the Payment Settings Tab. Of course, you need to be careful and make sure you are compliant, following Payment Card Industry (PCI) guidelines; go to https://www.pcicomplianceguide.org/faq/ to learn more. For example, in order to be PCI compliant, your QuickBooks needs to be password protected, and you need to have a secure, locked computer. While QuickBooks does let you store that information, if you are using some other type of credit card terminal to process the cards, that information is sometimes stored in that terminal. If so, you would not necessarily need to enter it in QuickBooks.

Setting up Vendor Lists

Vendor lists are very similar to customer lists. You can set up vendors directly from the vendor center, or when you are entering a new bill. You'll know if your vendor is already entered because, when you start typing the name in the bill, it will appear. If it doesn't, QuickBooks will ask you to add it.

The tabs in the vendor center are almost identical to the customer tabs, so I won't go over that again. The big difference between entering a customer and entering a vendor is that vendors don't have job tab because there's no reason for that. Instead, they have an additional tab that lets you record which expense account you want to populate once the vendor is selected.

For example, let's say you frequently go to Staples to buy office supplies. QuickBooks is set up so that if you enter "Staples" as the vendor, and you enter "office supplies" as the expense account, after a couple of times of seeing that, the program will tend to associate the two. But, if you later change it once, because maybe you used it for personal use and not business, QuickBooks may get a little bit confused. So, the next time you type it in, the program may leave everything blank because it isn't sure what expense you want to record.

To save time, under the additional information tab, you can enter an account that is associated with a given vendor. So, for example, you might put down that you always want any expense associated with Staples to be recorded as office supplies.

Employee Center

The Employee Center is where you can enter and manage employee information and time tracking. I'll get into more detail in a future chapter, but here is the high-level overview. You can process payroll within QuickBooks if you want, but you don't have to. You can also use a third-party payroll vendor for your payroll needs.

I primarily use the employee center for time tracking. For example, I have an accounting practice and I have employees who work in my practice. I set them up with a time tracking function where I can keep track of how much I'm paying them per hour to do work for me. I can also set them up on an invoice for the customer in the same item list, which shows how much I'm going to bill the customer. In one item, we're capturing both sides of the transaction.

Lead Center

The Lead Center is a Customer Relationship Management (CRM) tool for prospecting. If you want to gather information for prospects, you can enter it in this part of the program. It's not going to affect your financials, because it does not relate to any of the financial accounts. It just records preliminary information. You can also create estimates in the lead center. Those estimates will not affect your financials because it's not work that you've done yet.

By just clicking a button you can convert a prospect to customer by converting your estimate to an invoice. You can also modify your estimate and then convert it to an invoice.

Importing Data into Lists

QuickBooks offers several ways for you to add data to the system. When you are working with a lot of records, batch importing them may be the best option. Let's say that over the years you have built and maintained a long list of customers, and you have those records in an Excel spreadsheet. As long as you fill out the required field for each type of data import, e.g., customer or vendor list, you will be able to quickly populate the QuickBooks' database with your data.

Be mindful that you need to create a separate file for each type of data you want to import, i.e., do not mix customers and vendors data in the same file. More importantly, always back up your QuickBooks company file before each data import.

For more information, visit our video library:
http://www.OsserCPA.com/videos

Chapter 6

Managing Payables and Receivables

Cash flow is the lifeblood of every business. A recent study showed that 82% of all business failures are due to – not poor marketing or management – but poor cash flow. This chapter is about staying on top of your company's cash flow, by correctly using QuickBooks to manage accounts payable and accounts receivable.

In this chapter, I am going to cover:

- Accounts Payable
  - Paying Bills
  - Tracking Credit Card Charges
  - Reconciling Bank and Credit Card Statements
  - A/P Aging Report
- Accounts Receivable
  - Creating Sales Receipts or Invoices
  - Getting Paid
  - Recording Receipts
  - A/R Aging Report

Separating Personal and Business Accounts

Before I get into how you enter and track your payables (money you owe vendors) and receivables (money your clients owe you), I want to touch on the importance of separating your business and personal bank accounts and credit cards. No matter what type of business entity you have, it's really important to keep the funds separate. It protects you, and it also gives you an accurate picture of your business finances. If you happen to use a personal bank account, or you happen to occasionally charge business items on your personal card, we can still manage those items through journal entries.

It is a good practice to set up only your business-related accounts (not personal) in QuickBooks. Now let's look at how the money flows between payables and receivables in QuickBooks.

Accounts Payable

For cash flow purposes, as a business owner, it is essential that you understand to whom you are paying and when payment is due. In this section, you will learn how to enter and pay bills, monthly reconcile your accounts, and generate accounts payable reports to proactively manage the cash flow of your business.

Paying Bills

Two ways to handle vendor bills in QuickBooks are through Enter Bills and Write Checks. The major difference of the two is when bills are paid. For bills to be paid immediately, or if you are recording information for a bill that has already been paid, use the Write Checks feature; otherwise, use Enter Bills to record and pay a bill at a later time.

For example, when you receive your utility bill that's due the end of the month, you will use Enter Bills to record and track what you owe. When you pay it at the end of the month, use Pay Bills to clear the bill and print the check. Be mindful that the Enter Bills step is just recording the bill to show you owe the money; once you make the payment, the system will then show that the money has left your bank account.

On the other hand, say you bought supplies at Staples and had to pay for them immediately. In this case, you will use the Write Checks function to record the transaction. Use Write Checks also to process your EFT payments in QuickBooks.

When you pay bills via a check, you can either hand write checks, or you can order checks for your printer. Printing checks out of QuickBooks is easy, and it also saves time. You can order checks from QuickBooks or from a third-party vendor such as Costco at a very reasonable price. Just make sure to verify that the checks you order are compatible with QuickBooks.

Tracking Credit Card Charges

Frequently clients come to me about erroneous credit card transactions, because either the cards were improperly set up, or people used their personal credit cards to pay for business purchases. Hence I have devoted this section separately on how to properly record credit card transactions and pay your credit card bills.

If you have a few credit card transactions for your business, you may choose to just enter them manually in QuickBooks. However, if your credit card bills are more than a few pages long, it may be more convenient to use the download function that QuickBooks offers. Accessing this function varies depending upon the version of the QuickBooks you have installed, but the process is otherwise the same. First, look for Bank Feed from the menu option for a list of common bank and credit card companies. Then select your bank or financial institution and sign in with your username and password. Follow the onscreen instructions to download designated transactions into QuickBooks.

What I have noticed working with the transaction download is that the process may create duplicates, particularly payments. If you've already paid your bill, it might accidentally enter it a second time. This is where the reconciliation process (discussed later in this chapter) comes in, to double check and be sure that everything is in QuickBooks as it shows on your credit card or on your bank statements.

Another item to be aware of is that if you use the download function, say you frequently get gas at

ExxonMobil, and you go to one of ten different locations in town. Often each station has its own number, so you may have ten vendors in your system called ExxonMobil. If you choose to, you may merge all those transactions by reassigning them all under one vendor name.

Reconciling Bank and Credit Card Statements

Reconciliation, on a monthly basis, is one of the most important activities you should do for your business. By verifying your QuickBooks' records against your bank and credit card statements, you can be more assured from a cash flow perspective that you have sufficient funds on hand to pay your vendors.

I have had clients asking me in the past why they couldn't just use Excel or a notebook to manage their business accounts. One of the primary reasons is reconciliation. Reconciling your accounts involves comparing what transactions a third-party (usually your bank or credit card company) has recorded, to what your records show.

The process of reconciliation is fairly simple and straightforward where all that you're doing is going down the list, checking off the deposits made and checks written to your bank statement. When you are finished with the reconciliation, note that the difference must be zero, which means everything matches. If the difference is not zero, you will need to track down a mistake somewhere – did you forget to record a check? Did you make a typo in entering an amount? When the difference is zero, you will want to complete the reconciliation.

The same process happens with credit card reconciliations. One item to note is that QuickBooks may ask if you want to pay the credit card bill at the end of the reconciliation process. Since most people reconcile after payments have been made, more often than not, your answer will be "No."

A/P Aging Report

QuickBooks has many reports that offer business owners insights into their finances. The completeness and accuracy of the reports depend upon the completeness and accuracy of the data entered in QuickBooks.

The purpose of the Accounts Payable (A/P) Aging Report is to show to which vendors you owe money, the amount owed, and if the bills are current or past due. I suggest that this report be generated prior to doing a check run, so that you know who to pay.

Accounts Receivable

Enough about paying bills, now let's talk about how to properly record and receive money in QuickBooks.

Creating Sales Receipts or Invoices

It might sound trivial, but when exactly to record a sale is important, and it impacts your business financial statements. A sale is recorded when a project is complete or a sale is made. An exception to this rule is progress billing, which is sometimes used by construction companies.

There are two ways to records sales in QuickBooks – Enter Sales Receipts and Create Invoices.

Use Enter Sales Receipts when you are paid at the time you sell a product or service. For instance, say you are the owner of an ice cream parlor, or you sell goods at farmer's market on the weekends; as soon as a person buys a product from you, they pay you.

When working with clients who are set up to pay you in the future, you will use the Create Invoices function to record sales. By creating an invoice, QuickBooks automatically creates a receivable to keep track of money owed to you by a specific customer.

Getting Paid

When you send out the invoice to that customer and have received a payment for the invoice sent, you will record the payment using the Receive Payments feature. To do so in QuickBooks, select the customer who sent you a payment, say Company ABC sent in $1,000. In the payment box, enter the date you received the payment, the check number (if there is one), and the amount received. If there is only one invoice open, QuickBooks will automatically select it as the one to apply this payment to.

Let's say, however, that Company ABC has four outstanding invoices. QuickBooks is going to select the invoice with the invoice amount exactly matching the payment amount. If there is not an exact match, then QuickBooks will apply the payment amount to the outstanding invoices in order of date, i.e., older to newer invoices. You can always override what QuickBooks' selection and apply the payment to the invoice of your choice.

Recording Receipts

In situations of a pre-payment, that is a customer chooses to pay for products or services before work is performed, enter information about your customer in Receive Payments and record the pre-payment amount.

In the above example, notice that you will be able to record this as a receivable, but you will not have an invoice with which to associate this payment. Also note that the receivable report for this customer will have a negative balance, which is correct.

Depending upon how your business is structured, you may need to use a "holding account" to keep track of the payments you've received but have not deposited in the bank. This "holding account" is called Undeposited Funds in QuickBooks.

Suppose you own a retail store, and by the end of the day, you have 100 sales totaling $5,000. Now as you are a busy business owner, you do not go to the bank every day to make deposits, but in QuickBooks you need to have a way to record the sales receipts. By default, QuickBooks places all sales transactions in Undeposited Funds. When you are ready to deposit money in the bank, QuickBooks allows you to select all transactions matching the deposit amount and record them as one line item.

If you are a business owner who has low volume sales transactions, and you have a way of depositing funds on a regular basis, you can bypass using the Undeposited Funds feature and post receipts directly to your QuickBooks bank accounts.

A/R Aging Report

The Accounts Receivable (A/R) Aging Report, in summary and detail, provides business owners with an understanding of how they are at collecting money, which may positively or negatively affects the business's cash flow.

For instance, the A/R Aging Summary report shows who owes you money, how old the invoice is, and how many days overdue. You can see if your customers are current, which means the invoice is probably less than 30 days old. Or is the invoice a little bit older – 31 to 60 days, or 61 to 90, or over 90 days old? You want to know this, because you will want to follow up with customers who owe you money particularly if the receivables are over 90 days old. The older a receivable is, the less likely that you will be able to collect payment.

For more information, visit our video library:

http://www.OsserCPA.com/videos

Chapter 7

Reporting & Budgeting

The importance of business reporting is often overlooked or discussed as an afterthought, when in fact it is one of the most important reasons to use QuickBooks. The reason we enter and track all the data in QuickBooks is for us to evaluate, understand, and improve upon the health of our business. Once we understand how the business is doing, we can then set goals for the future by budgeting.

In this chapter, I am going to cover the following subject areas:

- Customizing Reports
  - Selecting Date Range
  - Accrual vs. Cash
  - Previous Period and Previous Year
  - Working with Filters
- The Top 12 Reports in QuickBooks
  - Profit and Loss / Income Statement
  - Profit and Loss by Class
  - Profit and Loss by Job

- Income and Expense Graphs
- Balance Sheet
- Accounts Receivable Summary
- Average Days to Pay
- Sales by Rep
- Accounts Payable Aging Summary
- Payroll Reports
- Audit Trail
- Budgeting

The purpose of budgeting is to set goals for the coming year by projecting future revenues and expenses. One of my clients is a successful Realtor with whom I have worked for many years. She utilizes budgeting to project sales goals for both herself and her employees, as well as estimating what her future expenses would be if those revenue projections were met. As a result, her business has grown every year for the past seven years. She didn't always meet her goals, but she consistently increased her sales.

What Reports Can Tell You

In an earlier chapter, I mentioned that QuickBooks is a scorecard that shows how you're doing over a period of time. If you know all of the data you've entered is accurate and up-to-date, you can then run reports and drill down into the numbers to make sure your business is operating as it should.

The Desktop Pro or Premier versions of QuickBooks have more than 100 reports pre-programmed in the software. My advice is to spend time playing with some of the reports, because you can't mess anything up and you'll get an idea of what they show you.

Customizing Reports

The list of reports available in QuickBooks varies based upon the versions you use. Most of the time, you can customize QuickBooks reports to suit your specific business needs. For example, you can include your company's logo in invoices you send to clients. You can add or remove form fields, change font type, size, and colors to give you the look and feel that you want your business to represent.

The most commonly customized fields in QuickBooks are date range, method of accounting (accrual vs. cash), and date range comparison.

Selecting Date Range

Just about every QuickBooks report lets you set a data range to view information relating to a specific period of time. For some reports, such as the Profit & Loss statement, you want to see a date range of a month or a year to understand your profitability over that month or year. Other reports, for example the Balance Sheet report, are generated for a single point of time.

Accrual vs. Cash

When running most reports, it is critical that you know whether you have selected cash-based or accrual-based accounting as the framework of the report. Why is it important to check this first? Because the results may differ dramatically between the two methods. You can select the method you wish to use as the default for all reports in the QuickBooks preference tab.

Comparing Previous Periods and Previous Years

From time to time, as a business owner, you will want to know how your business is doing this month/quarter/year compared to the previous month/quarter/year. Let's say you are reviewing your Profit & Loss for the year 2017. It would be very helpful to compare it to your 2016 profit and loss, and with this feature both years will print side by side on the same Profit& Loss Report.

Working with Filters

Filters are a very useful feature, because they help narrow down your search and give you only the data that you need. The Customize Report function in QuickBooks, under the Reports menu, allows you to set filters to further refine your search. Some common fields include the names of Vendor(s) or Customer(s) Sales Representatives at your company. Once you filter the information that is relevant to your needs, you can tell QuickBooks to memorize the report you just created, so you can easily run them again with the same criteria in the future.

The Top 12 Reports in QuickBooks

While there are many report options, here are a list of 12 reports that I use most often for my business and my clients.

Profit and Loss / Income Statement

Profit and Loss (P&L) and Income Statement are essentially the same report. If you report on a cash basis, you are creating a profit and loss report (which is what most small businesses do). Accrual-based firms generate income statements. Both reports show how your business is doing over a specific period of time, such as a month or a year. They will tell you how much revenue and how many expenses you have for that period.

Once you determine how to set up the report, take a close look at it, particularly if it's your first time creating it. You can click "cash" and run the report, then go back and click "accrual" and run the report again. You'll see a difference if you have a fair amount of receivables, including open invoices that haven't been paid yet. On the accrual basis, as soon as you invoice a client, it's going to show as income. On the cash basis, it doesn't show until you receive the money.

You can also compare your expenses under both approaches. On an accrual basis, you'd want to be sure you're capturing all the expenses – not just the bills you've paid. Work with a CPA to verify that you're not missing any important expenses. If you are, your CPA can help you adjust entries and accrue for any expenses that hadn't been entered. If you only had 11 utility bills for the year and there should be 12, we'll have to do a little bit of extra work and accrue for that twelfth month.

On the cash basis, if you have entered all of your transactions and reconciled your Balance Sheet Accounts, you are ready to run the Profit and Loss report. The Profit and Loss is one statement that your CPA will use to prepare your Income Tax Return. There will be some adjustments that go on the tax form, which I'll cover in a later chapter.

Profit and Loss by Class

In addition to the standard Profit and Loss report, there are a few variations. Profit and Loss by Class, and Profit and Loss by Job, are two of those most frequently used by business owners. For instance, I use the Profit and Loss by Class report for people who may have more than one location or operate their business in multiple states. The class functionality lets you see all the income and all expenses per state or location.

Let's say you are a Realtor and you sell houses in Virginia and in Maryland. The class tracking function will allow you to identify and track whether your revenue and expenses pertain to Virginia or to Maryland. You would then run the Profit and Loss by Class report, where you would determine your profitability in each state. QuickBooks tracks any transactions without a specific Class, e.g. VA or MD in this example, as "Uncategorized." You can easily assign any uncategorized activity to its proper class.

Profit and Loss by Job

The Profit and Loss by Job report shows your net income by job and/or project. Any expense relating to a specific customer or job is going to appear in that report along with the income. I use this report a great deal for my clients in the construction industry, but it can also be useful in almost any business. For example, this report is very beneficial for real estate agents who want to see how much income they netted on individual home sales, comparing one deal to the next and learning how to be more profitable on future transactions.

Income & Expense Graph

Graphs are visual representations of your financial data on an accrual basis. QuickBooks offers graph choices including pie charts, bar graphs, and line graphs.

One graph that I use frequently is the income and expense graph. This graph is useful if you have different jobs or work with a lot of different customers. You'll see a nice bar graph that shows how much money you made or lost, per project or per job, and have the ability to drill down to the details.

When creating graphs in QuickBooks, you are only able to see them on an accrual basis. They are not available if you are using cash-based accounting. You've heard the saying, "A picture is worth a thousand words." Graphs are visually appealing, offer the big-picture viewpoint, and are easy to understand. Gaining deeper insight into how your business is doing, however, will require you to look at the details behind the graphs.

Balance Sheet

A balance sheet shows your assets, liabilities, and equity. While the profit and loss report shows business performance over time, a balance sheet is a snapshot of how your business is doing at a specific point in time. It's customary to run the balance sheet at the end of a year. On December 31, it will show what your assets are minus your liabilities. What is left is your equity, which is what you have in the business.

The balance sheet is a crucial report. We use it to report fixed assets — you want to be sure all of your fixed assets appear under the asset section, because you will be depreciating them. The same goes for your liabilities, such as your truck loan.

You run the report and scan it for accuracy. Like other reports, you can drill down into the detail of the balance sheet. The balance sheet is also frequently used to prepare your income tax return.

Accounts Receivable Summary

As I mentioned in Chapter 6, one of the biggest challenges small businesses have is cash flow, and that's where the accounts receivable reports come in. The accounts receivable summary shows us who owes us money and how old the invoices are – current, 31 to 60 days old, 61 to 90, or even over 90 days old. If an account receivable is current, there's a very good probability you're going to get paid, particularly if this is a client with whom you have a long history.

However, as people owe you money for a longer period of time, the likelihood of getting paid decreases. We want to analyze this. As you are doing billing, print this report out to see how old invoices are. If some are more than 30 days old for example, you should call the customer and see what is happening and find out when you can expect payment.

Average Days to Pay

Average Days to Pay is a really cool report, although most people are not aware that it exists in QuickBooks. When setting up a new customer in QuickBooks, you determine payment terms: cash on delivery, Net 30, credit etc. Say that you have a client who only works with you once or twice a year, and you're deciding on the terms you want to offer. This report weighs the amount the client owes you and how long it's been since they paid you. Pull up this report and, if this customer always pays promptly, offer them good terms. If you have another customer who always takes 153 days to pay, you may choose to be less generous in the payment terms you offer.

Sales by Rep

The Sales by Rep report is useful for anyone who has a sales team, particularly if the sales reps are paid on commission. I use this report for real estate teams with multiple real estate agents, and law firms that have multiple attorneys billing clients.

The term Rep here is used in a generic sense, which can represent a list of sales representatives, partners in a law firm, or basically anyone whose sales activities you want to track on your financial statements. For example, a law firm with eight attorneys can run this report to see how much money each of the eight attorneys brought in for any period of time — a day, a month, or a year.

Accounts Payable Aging Summary

As discussed in Chapter 6 – Managing Payables and Receivables, the Accounts Payable Aging Summary report tells you who you owe money to, and when payments are due. If any payments are past due, this report shows you how late it is, i.e., the age of a payment due. Again, knowing this information allows you to effectively prioritize your bill paying process.

Payroll Reports

I discussed the subject of payroll earlier in this book. My preference is that my clients use a third-party vendor who specializes in processing payroll rather than them doing it through QuickBooks. If you do choose to use the QuickBooks Payroll module, you'll find 10 to 15 of the most common reports for payroll. So rest assured you can pull out all the information you need.

Audit Trail

The audit trail is a way of keeping track of who has entered a particular transaction or ran a specific report. This is especially important if you have more than one person working in QuickBooks. You may also have an outside bookkeeper or a CPA working in your QuickBooks file as well. If you come across a transaction and want to know who entered it or changed it, you can find out with this report. The audit trail is where the software timestamps and tracks actions by who logged in and made every entry in QuickBooks.

Budgeting

Another powerful report that is sometimes overlooked by users is budgeting. Just as

QuickBooks can look backward at the data you've entered and give you reports on how you've been doing in the past and up to this point, it can also produce reports that will help you budget, project, and plan going forward into the future.

Very few businesses do budgeting, but almost all really should. Everyone has great goals and visions. They want to get somewhere, succeed in their businesses, and enjoy happily ever after. Budgeting is a tool that will help you reach those goals.

Budgets give you something to shoot for, a target to which you can compare your actual results. Before you can get any insightful information for planned versus actual, you will need to set up a budget. I suggest that you work with a CPA to help you analyze your business needs and establish a reasonable budget.

For more information, visit our video library:
http://www.OsserCPA.com/videos

Chapter 8

Working with Inventory

For business owners with products to sell, knowing how to work with the inventory module in QuickBooks is essential.

Activating the inventory module in QuickBooks is fairly straightforward. In the QuickBooks desktop version, all you need to do is edit your company preferences to enable the use of inventory and purchase orders. There are, however, inventory specific concepts, listed below, that I want to point out in this chapter to ensure you are using the inventory function as it is intended.

- Creating Product Inventory
- Valuation
- Sales Price
- Using Purchase Orders (POs)

In this chapter, we will discuss Tim's Toy Store, a fictional store based in Busy town, USA. Now Tim is eccentric; he only carries one product in his entire store – the game of Monopoly. Tim purchases Monopoly from a distributor, marks up the price of the game and sells it in his store.

Creating Product Inventory

Inventory is a three-sided transaction. What does that mean? When Tim buys the Monopoly games from his supplier, he is purchasing inventory. When he purchases the games, two things happen: his inventory goes up, and his cash goes down.

Now, a customer comes into the store and buys a Monopoly game, and Tim records the transaction. In QuickBooks, the inventory goes down, and the cost of goods sold goes up by the same amount. Cost of goods sold is an expense associated with the products business owners sell. Additionally, Tim receives revenue from the sale of the game, so the store's cash and revenue go up by the price customer paid for the Monopoly game.

You can see there are a lot of steps associated with this sales transaction. Therefore, when you set up the product inventory, it is critical to complete the necessary fields correctly. In QuickBooks, this is accomplished by going to your Item List, selecting a new item under Type and selecting Inventory Part. From there you will specify the type of products in the inventory, purchase information such as cost, and cost of goods sold account, sales information like sales price, tax code, and income account, and inventory information, e.g., asset account, re-order number, and total value.

Valuing Inventory

If the price Tim pays for the purchase of Monopoly inventory item never changes, determining the value of the inventory is simple – just multiply the number of units on the shelf by the price Tim pays. But prices usually fluctuate, meaning inventory of a single product will represent a mix of different purchase prices. How can you put a value on that?

Three common ways for valuing inventory are: 1. Average Cost, 2. First In First Out (FIFO), 3. Last In First Out (LIFO)

Average cost weighs the average price you pay. Let's say Tim's Toy Store buys ten Monopoly games from their supplier at $5 each, and then buys another ten games a month later at $6 each. Using the average cost inventory value method, QuickBooks would take the average of Tim's inventory. In this example $5 x 10 = $50 for the first order and $6 x 10 = $60 for the second order. The total inventory is now $110. If you divide the total amount by 20 monopoly games, the average Cost of Goods sold (COGS) is $5.50 each.

Using the FIFO (First In First Out) method of inventory valuation, the first Monopoly game that Tim purchases will be the first product that Tim sells. The COGS for the first 10 games Tim sells would be $5 each, and the COGS of the next 10 games that Tim sells would be $6 each.

The noted difference, as you see in this example, is the COGS per unit, i.e., $5.50 under average cost and $5 when using FIFO. If Tim sells the Monopoly game for $10 each, FIFO will yield a higher profitability than using the average cost method.

So, what about LIFO, or Last In First Out? Before you get too excited about this, I must tell you that QuickBooks does not use LIFO for tracking COGS. But, just to complete the loop on this, with LIFO, the last piece of inventory purchased will be sold first with the COGS of $6.

OK, so how do you select which method to use? You don't. The Desktop version of QuickBooks only allows you to use the average cost method, and the Online version of QuickBooks only uses the FIFO method. This is problematic when you decide to switch from the desktop version of QuickBooks to the online version, or the other way around. Should this happen in your case, I suggest that you speak to your CPA for assistance.

Sales Price

Business owners such as Tim from Tim's Toy Store usually set the sales price of all their products. In QuickBooks, you have the ability to set profit margin on each product that you sell. The profit margin can be a percentage of the COGS or a fixed amount, both of which can be adjusted at any time.

Let's say Tim decides to establish a fixed sales price of $10 per Monopoly game that he sells. As mentioned before, his cost to purchase the games from his supplier may fluctuate from time to time. Between the first and second group of 10 games that Tim purchased, his cost went from $5 each to $6 each. With a fixed sales price, Tim would be selling the Monopoly game at $10 each regardless of COGS, thus making less of a profit as his costs go up.

As a result, Tim may prefer to add a profit margin percentage on top of COGS. This percentage can be set product by product. Let's say Tim wants to make a 100% profit on every Monopoly game he sells. By designating this in QuickBooks, when his COGS is $5, the sales price of the game will be $10. When the COGS increased to $5.50, his sales price then will increase to $11.

One major drawback to setting a profit margin percentage is that, when your COGS fluctuates over short period of time, your products' retail prices will rapidly go up and down, causing your customers to pay different prices on different days for the same product.

Purchase Orders (POs)

Not everyone needs to create purchase orders, but it is a good practice to use them. A purchase order is a non-posting transaction, which means when you create it, it does not affect your financials.

The purpose of creating a purchase order is to track exactly what you order. On the purchase order, you may specify an item number, product description, price, quantity, etc. This is very important, because when the bill comes in from the supplier you gave a purchase order to, you will have a way to verify that you received the right product, with the right quantity, and at the right price. Additionally, when your supplier accepts your purchase order, the order becomes a legally binding document, which protects both sides.

For more information, visit our video library:
http://www.OsserCPA.com/videos

Chapter 9

Your Business and Your Taxes

At the time that I am finalizing this book for print, a new tax bill has been signed into law for 2018. This new law is not just a tweak but rather a large-scale tax reform that will affect you and your businesses. The last time a reform of this magnitude was passed was 30 years ago under President Regan.

I have studied this new tax law in depth, and I can tell you that it is very different from the old law, and it is far from simple. If anything, it is probably more complicated to understand. The House and the Senate were in such a hurry to pass the bill that they knowingly passed it with many technical issues; they plan on amending some of the issues that they are aware of in early 2018. Details of this new bill should become clearer in the months ahead.

This new law has major ramifications for business owners. You should speak to a qualified CPA to discuss your unique situation and how this law may affect your taxes.

In this Chapter, I'm going to cover:

- Keeping track of your receipts; I recommend getting a scanner.
- Common business deductions and how they are treated:
  - Automobile – Standard Rate vs Actual Costs
  - Home Office – Two methods
  - Business Travel
  - Meals & Entertainment
  - Depreciation
  - Insurance – Health Insurance and Life Insurance
  - Business Gifts
- Tax Saving Strategies
  - Sole Proprietors and Single Member LLCs
  - Multi-Member LLCs
  - S Corporations
  - C Corporations
- Summary of Changes in the 2018 Tax Reform

Keeping Track of Your Receipts

As a business owner, you're allowed to deduct business expenses from your revenue to reduce your taxable income. In order to deduct them, you need to prove the expenses are ordinary and necessary for your business. Keeping receipts and meticulous records as documentation of your business expenses makes things easier when it comes to year-end filings.

Have you noticed that the receipts you get are always printed on flimsy paper? After a week or two, they've already begun to fade and you risk losing some of the information on them. If you ever get audited, you will need those receipts as proof for what you purchased. Audits never happen right away; they take place months or years down the road. If your receipts are unreadable now, imagine what they will look like three years from now.

If your receipts are illegible three years from now, even if you have them all, you will not have the documentation needed to support your deductions. One way to keep good quality records of your receipts is to invest in a scanner.

Which scanner is right for you will depend on the volume of receipts you need to scan. Find one you like and start scanning your receipts immediately. You can then store them electronically, and the IRS will accept those as documentations. It's easy and you're not losing any of that valuable information.

Also, if you happen to scan the receipts as PDFs, which I normally like to do, you can attach them to invoices and bills in QuickBooks. There is a paperclip icon that you click and just attach the file. That way, the receipt is always right there for you.

Common Business Deductions

Automobile Deduction

One of the most common expenses I get questions on is what to do with the business automobile. How do I deduct it? How is it treated?

To answer these questions, we first have to look at your automobile and find out how much you actually use it for business. Having a business automobile means tracking miles. There are several apps out there that help you with the tracking. You could also keep a logbook or a calendar of when and where you went, and how many miles you traveled. You just need some type of written documentation, so we know how much you traveled for business. From that, we determine the total mileage on the car for the year, and how much of your travel for the year was business versus personal.

If you tend to use your car at least 50% or more for business, then it may make sense to depreciate your car. Say you buy a new vehicle for $30,000, the government will not allow you to expense the whole $30,000 in the year of purchase, rather you will need to capitalize the car and depreciate it over many years. Based on IRS guidelines for depreciation, there are several options for how to depreciate your business vehicle. Speak to your

CPA about the best depreciation method for you to use

Another area that we look at with the car is operating expenses. If you depreciate the car, your costs of operation — gasoline, oil changes, repairs and maintenance, car washes — are also business expenses, based on the percentage that you use it for business versus personal. If we determine that you use your vehicle 80% of the time for business, we can write off 80% of the operating expenses.

When you are entering these vehicle expenses into QuickBooks, be sure to include the entire expense. Your CPA should correctly adjust the deductible amounts on your tax return to reflect the percentage that you used the vehicle for business verses personal.

Alternatively, you can deduct your mileage on the car, and that is often a lot easier to do. If you're not depreciating, you don't have to track those extra expenses for gas, maintenance, and etc. You still need your mileage log. What you're doing instead is taking a fixed fee per mile that the government sets, which is currently $0.545/mile in 2018. You multiply your business mileage by that IRS rate, and that is your deduction for the automobile expense.

Home Office Deduction

To be eligible for a home office deduction, you need to have a place in your home that you use regularly and exclusively for conducting business. It can't be your dining room table, where you work but you also have dinner. You must have a part of the house where you regularly and exclusively *only* do work.

The good news is this can be, but it does not have to be, a separate room. It could be a large room that has a desk, file cabinet, and computer in the corner. If you regularly and exclusively only do work there, that can be your home office.

If you have an employer who has provided you another place where your work can be performed, you would not be able to deduct your home office. Also, owners of S-Corporations (which will be explained later in this chapter) are not eligible for the home office deduction. If you qualify for a home office deduction, you are able to start tracking business miles from when you leave your home for a client visit.

So if you qualify for a home office deduction, how do you record it in QuickBooks? How do you record it on your tax return? I do not recommend that my clients enter their home office activity in QuickBooks, but rather collect the necessary information and present it to their CPA at tax time.

There are two methods for claiming a home office deduction; a traditional method and a simplified method. The traditional method requires a lot more work, and you have to account for a number of things, including; depreciation of the area of your home used as an office, documentation for utilities used, real estate taxes paid, home mortgage interest payments, and the recapture of depreciation of that portion of your home upon sale of the house. Because of this, in 2013, a simplified method was developed where, if you qualify for a home office deduction, you can multiply the number of square feet (maximum 300 square feet) by $5, and that is your deduction.

Because of recent changes in the 2018 tax law, I expect that home office deductions will be a hot topic of discussion, and you should discuss with your CPA to see which method makes most sense for you.

Business Travel

Expenses for business travel are an area where people seem to think they can write off everything. They say, "Well, I was on travel" to explain an expense. And I'll say, "That's great, but what did you spend the money on?" We still need to break it down, for a variety of reasons.

One reason is that, even though you're on business travel, your meals are only 50% deductible. You need to break that down, and you need to know that it's not going to be called travel, it's called meals. There are other things that you really want to see also, just for internal tracking. How much did you spend on airfare, or on mileage if you drove, or on the hotel, or on parking?

It's generally a best practice to break these things down, rather than calling everything travel. The only items that I generally put under travel are hotel and airfare.

Meals and Entertainment (M&E)

You may be aware that if you take a client out to eat, or you have a business purpose for meeting over a meal, you can deduct that from your taxes. Unfortunately, you only get to deduct half of your actual cost.

You can thank Wall Street in the early 1980s for this. You may remember hearing about the three-martini lunches. A lot of stockbrokers on Wall Street would go out for very expensive lunches in the afternoon. The joke was they'd have three martinis, spend a lot of money, and say it's all a business expense. Congress got tired of people abusing the system, so while they still allow it, they decided you can only deduct half of your meals and entertainment.

With the new 2018 tax law, meals will still be deductible at 50%, but entertainment will no longer be allowed as a business expense deduction. This means that tickets to the game with your clients will no longer be a deductible business expense.

In the past, Meals & Entertainment was typically classified at one expense category. Starting in 2018, you will need to break this into two separate expense accounts, one called meals, and the other, entertainment.

When you record a meal expense or entertainment expenses in your business records, you want to put in the full amount that you spent. Your CPA will do a computation when they prepare your taxes to adjust your expense to 50% for meals or to non-deductible for entertainment.

Depreciation

Depreciation is also something that confuses many of my clients. I generally enter depreciation into QuickBooks for my clients after I prepare their income tax returns. You should work with your tax preparer on entering depreciation into your QuickBooks program.

Insurance

There are two common insurance questions I frequently address with small business owners. The first one is health insurance. Generally speaking, payment of employees' health insurance premiums is a deductible business expense. If you are set up as a Sole Proprietor, an LLC, or an S Corporation, then deduction of the owner's health insurance does not happen at the business entity, but rather it flows through as a deduction on your personal tax return. As a C corporation, the business would claim the tax deduction for the owners' health insurance premiums, and it would not flow to the owner's personal tax return.

Properly recording health insurance premiums for the owners of S Corporations involves a few more steps, so work with a payroll company that has experience processing payroll for the owners of S Corporations.

The payment of life insurance premiums is generally not deductible, because it is usually a personal expense. If you die, your family – not your business – gets the payout from of the policy. The exception is if you buy "key man" life insurance. With a key man policy, if something happens to you as an owner of the business, the insurance payout goes to your business to recruit and hire someone to fill your shoes, so the business can continue operating.

Business Gifts

Business gifts involve the giving of something of value by a taxpayer to their clients or other business associates, made in the course of the taxpayer's trade or business. Deductibility of business gifts are limited to $25 per person or entity, plus shipping. So if you spend $100 on a gift that you bought from a store, you would put the entire $100 expense in QuickBooks. Your tax preparer would later reduce the deductibility of that gift to $25.

An interesting tax loophole that could help you deduct the entire $100, rather than the $25 gift limit, involves treating the item as advertising rather than as a gift. How do you do that? Well let's say you just purchased a home and your realtor gives you a barbeque set as an appreciation for doing business with them. It is a beautiful barbeque set and it prominently displays your realtor's logo, which is permanently attached to the set. This is no longer a gift from your realtor. It can now be considered a promotional item that the realtor is using to obtain business in the future.

Tax Saving Strategies

With the tax reform act of 2018, many business owners will pay less federal tax on their share of their business' profits. If you file as a Sole Proprietor, or a pass-through entity such as an LLC, or an S-Corporation, and your Taxable Income (TI) from your Form 1040 is below the required threshold, which for 2018 are $315,000 if you are Married Filing Jointly (MFJ) or below $157,500 if you are a Single (S) filer, then you would receive a 20% reduction of your Qualified Business Income (QBI) for Federal tax purposes. If your income is above the threshold amount listed above, it is still possible to receive a deduction of up to 20%.

For example, if you are a Single Member LLC making $100,000 in taxable income in 2018, and if you file your 1040 return as MFJ with a total TI of $210,000, then you would qualify for this tax benefit. Your $100,000 of business income would be reduced by 20% and you would only pay Federal tax on $80,000 of your business income.

Here's another example. Let's say you are a Single Member LLC still making $100,000 of taxable business income, and you are married filing jointly, but your TI is now $500,000. Your income would be above the $315,000 threshold in 2018. However, you may still qualify for a tax reduction, as much as 20%. You should work with a qualified individual such as a CPA to help determine if you qualify, so you can maximize your business tax deductions.

If you are a C Corporation, then in lieu of the 20% deduction listed above, you will receive a reduced tax rate of 21% and no longer be subject to the Alternative Minimum Tax (AMT) at a corporate level.

Sole Proprietor and Single Member LLC

If you are a Sole Proprietor, you are filing a Schedule C for your business as part of your personal tax return. As a Single Member LLC, you also file the same Schedule C on your personal return unless you elect to be treated differently. Filing a Schedule C is the easiest of the business tax returns for you to file. Not that it's easy, but it's easier than some of the other options.

If you enter your transactions correctly and reconcile your accounts properly, QuickBooks will do a great job providing you with the data that is needed to complete your business tax return. Subtract your expenses from your revenue, and make some modifications to address items that may not be fully deductible. What remains is the taxable income from your business. This business taxable income is subject to Federal Insurance Contributions Act, better known as the FICA tax, which pays for Social Security and Medicare. If you were employed by a business, you would pay for ½ of this FICA tax through W-2 withholdings, and your employer would pay for the other ½ of the FICA tax. Since you are self-employed, you will be acting as both employee and employer subject to the full 100% of the FICA tax. The FICA tax that is due from your Schedule C income is calculated and included in your 1040 tax return.

Now, if you and your spouse work in the business together, and you are both owners of the business, you are a partnership. You would generally file a tax form (not a Schedule C) separate from your personal tax return, known as a partnership Form 1065.

There is a loophole in the law where spouses can have a qualified joint venture, which allows them to each file their own Schedule C instead of filling a separate tax return on a Form 1065.

Multi-Member LLCs

If you are a Multi-Member LLC, by default, you file a tax Form 1065. You're still tracking your revenue and expenses, but there are also a lot of additional things that need to be tracked as part of the tax return, such as reconciling your return against your balance sheet and having the individual owners keep track of their basis.

The tax Form 1065 then produces Form K-1 for each owner of the Multi-Member LLC. The K-1 form breaks down the percentage of the taxable income which is based on the business operating agreement. For example, let's say you have a business with a taxable income of $100,000, and your share is 10%. The K-1 form is going to list your share of the business income as $10,000. The $10,000 income from your K-1 form would then be included in your personal return where you would pay your Federal taxes on your business income. You usually also would pay FICA taxes on the Form 1040 for this business income.

S Corporations

Prior to 2018, many entities elected to be taxed as an S Corporation. One big advantage of doing so is that the profits of the S Corporation are not subject to FICA tax. While this is still the case, Congress is considering changing the law to make profits of an S Corporation subject to FICA tax.

As the owner of an S Corporation, you will need to pay yourself a fair and reasonable salary through payroll, and you will receive a W-2 at the end of the year. Now by doing this, it creates an issue for your S Corporation. Remember I mentioned earlier that an S Corporation is a pass-through entity and could receive a deduction of 20% on business income when qualified. Well that 20% deduction only applies to the business profits, and it does not include your salary in the deduction.

Let's revisit with Tim at his business, Tim's Toy Store. Tim has elected to be taxed as an S Corporation. In 2018, Tim determined that as the Owner and President of Tim's Toy Store that $85,000 was a fair and reasonable salary for himself. Supposing Tim's taxable net income for his S Corporation was $60,000 for 2018, and supposing Tim is married and filing jointly on his personal tax return and meets the threshold requirements. Tim would receive a deduction of 20% of his QBI.

Tim does not receive any of the 20% tax deduction on his payroll earnings. So, what is to prevent Tim from paying himself no salary and then claiming that his QBI is $145,000, which would maximize his 20% deduction on this business income? That is not allowed, because Tim MUST pay himself a fair and reasonable salary. Paying himself nothing would not meet the IRS requirements of a fair and reasonable salary.

If Tim elected to be an LLC instead of an S Corporation, he would not have this problem, because Tim would not receive a payroll as the owner of an LLC, and he would be able to take the 20% deduction on his entire taxable income of $145,000.

C Corporations

Effective 2018, the tax rate for C Corporations has been reduced to 21%, and the AMT has been repealed for C Corporations. Let's take a detailed look at C Corporations and taxes.

Unlike the other business entities we discussed, where profits are taxed to the owners of the business, a C Corporation pays its own taxes. So, the good news is that C Corporations will pay a fairly low tax at 21%. But how do you take money out of a C Corporation?

One way is to pay yourself a salary for working in the C Corporation. The wages are taxed as ordinary income on your personal tax return just as if you worked for someone else and received a paycheck, so there is not necessarily any tax benefit for doing so.

Another way to withdraw money from your C Corporation is in the form of dividends. Now issuing dividends will require some tax planning, because when you receive the dividends, you need to record them on your individual tax return and will probably have to pay tax on your Form 1040. Dividends are taxed between 0% - 23.8% depending on your AGI and taxable income. If you are planning on using this entity for your small business, you and your CPA need to do some advance tax planning.

Summary of Changes in the 2018 Tax Reform

The 2018 Tax Reform Law will bring about many changes for both individuals and business owners. In this section, I summarize some of the major changes to the law. But bear in mind that there are many technical issues that the House and the

Senate are fixing with a Technical Corrections Bill that will be introduced in January 2018.

First let's look at some of the major items that the tax reform was supposed to address. You can determine for yourself if the goals were accomplished.

1. The new lower tax rates for individuals are set to sunset in 2025 and go back to the rates from 2017, while the tax reduction of C Corporations to 21% is permanent.
2. The politicians wanted to make the new law simple enough that most people could file their return on a postcard style tax form. What they have done is make it more difficult to itemize your deductions so fewer individuals will file a Schedule A, going forward.
3. The repeal of the Alternative Minimum Tax (AMT) has been enacted for C Corporations but not for individuals. The AMT exemptions have been increased and indexed to inflation so fewer people will be subject to this additional tax, but it still exists for many individuals.
4. The new tax rates have been changed to: 10%, 12%, 22%, 24%, 32%, 35%, and 37%.
5. There is a penalty still for tax year 2018 for not having health insurance coverage meeting the Affordable Care Act requirements; this requirement will be removed in 2019.

The new tax reform law mostly goes into effect in 2018, and you will notice the changes when you file your tax returns in 2019. Because there are so many sweeping changes, I suggest that individuals and business owners begin tax planning to minimize the burden.

Here are some of the major changes that will affect individuals:

1. There are no more personal exemptions. So, in 2017 when you prepared your individual tax return, you were allowed to deduct $4,050 for each person who qualified. Going forward this no longer is deductible. If you were a family of 4 in 2017 and you did not meet the phase-out thresholds, then you would have been able to reduce your taxable income by $16,200. In 2018, you will not receive any deduction for personal exemptions.

2. The Standard Deduction has increased to $12,000 for Single Filers (S), $24,000 for Married Filing Jointly (MFJ), and $18,000 for Head of Household (HOH). This is up from $6,350 (S), $12,700 (MFJ), and $9,300(HOH) in 2017. This change was apparently made to adjust for the loss of deducting personal exemptions, and as a way to encourage individuals to take the standard deduction instead of the itemized deduction. Seniors over age 65 or blind individuals can take an additional $1,300 standard deduction.

3. Changes for individuals who itemize their deductions:
    a. Medical Deductions are allowed subject to a 7 ½ % of AGI threshold in 2018, which will increase to 10% of AGI threshold in 2019.
    b. State and Local Property Taxes (SALT) will be limited to a maximum of $10,000. Personal Property Taxes on things such as automobiles will no longer be allowed to be deducted.
    c. Mortgages established before 12/15/17 were grandfathered in, allowing you to deduct the interest on up to $1,000,000 of indebtedness. Loans that were made after 12/15/17 will be limited to $750,000 of indebtedness for a tax write-off purposes. Lines of Credit on your home will be difficult to deduct, subject to home equity indebtedness.
    d. Charity contribution will still be deductible with a maximum deduction of 60% of AGI. This is up from 50% of AGI in 2017. Many charities are concerned that this new tax law will entice many to take the standard deduction rather than itemize, which could lead to less contributions going to your favorite charity.
    e. Miscellaneous Deductions subject to 2% of AGI have been removed, so you can no

longer deduct unreimbursed employer expenses or expenses from your financial advisor or accountant. This also means that for individuals who have a hobby, they are required to record and pay tax on all of their revenue but are no longer allowed to deduct any of the expenses associated with that hobby.

   f. Casualty Losses will no longer be deductible, unless it occurs in a Presidentially Declared Disaster Area.

4. If you have children subject to the Kiddie Tax, the taxing structure has changed where the earned income with be taxed at an individual single rate, but the investment income will be taxed at the trust return rates.

5. Child Care Credit has been increased to $2,000 per child under the age of 17 with a limit on the refundable amount of $1,400, and an AGI phase-out of $400,000 for MFJ. This will help many people off set not being able to deduct exemptions.

6. No new contributions will be allowed for the Coverdell IRA. Instead, you can now use your 529 plan for K-12 and college. You will be able to roll your Coverdell into a 529 plan tax free. The 529 plan cannot be used for home schooling.

7. The estate tax exclusion will increase to $10,000,000 for the next five years and then revert back to 2017 levels

8. You can no longer deduct moving expenses, and if your employer pays for your moving expenses, it will now be included in your income, and taxed. Moving expenses are still deductible for military personnel.
9. For any divorce proceedings that commence after 12/31/2018, alimony paid will not be deductible.

Keeping up with the tax law changes and figuring out how the changes may impact your business and you as an individual is a challenge. Tax planning is also crucial to ensure you are staying on top of your personal finances. Because of the complexity and nuances involved in the new tax reform, I suggest that you speak to your CPA early to plan accordingly.

For more information, visit our video library:
http://www.OsserCPA.com/videos

Chapter 10

Retirement Planning for Business Owners

In my practice, I have found that as small business owners become more successful and established, they are ready to discuss retirement planning. They love what they're doing, but at some point they want to retire. Although the topics I'm about to discuss here are not particularly related to QuickBooks, enough people have approached me in the past about saving for retirement that I decided to devote a separate chapter to the subject.

In this chapter, I will discuss ways to save for retirement and tax saving for doing so. Specifically, I will compare and contrast the following types of retirement accounts:

- IRA
- Roth IRA
- Simple IRA
- SEP IRA
- 401(k)
- Solo 401(k) with Profit Sharing
- Self-Directed IRA

There are multiple retirement plans available to small business owners, and many of them save you money on taxes in addition to providing you with a nest egg for retirement. I'm going to touch on the most common retirement plans. This is by no means an all-inclusive list, rather these are the plans with which many people are familiar.

IRA

IRA stands for Individual Retirement Account. An IRA can be opened by anyone with earned income who is under 70 ½ years old. You do not have to be a business owner to open this account. In order to make tax deductible contributions to your IRA, your income must be below certain Adjusted Gross Income (AGI) thresholds. Please check with your CPA to verify if your IRA qualifies as a deductible IRA. The maximum you can contribute to an IRA is $5,500 per year (as of 2017). If you're over age 50, you can contribute as much as $6,500 a year.

If you have a spouse who is under 70 ½, your spouse can also contribute to the IRA as long as one of you has an earned income. So if you and your spouse both contribute to the IRA, and if you both meet the income requirements for deductibility, you can reduce your gross income by $11,000, which is going to save most people many thousands of dollars in taxes.

Another advantage of an IRA is that the money grows tax-deferred. What that means is that if you're in your 30s now and you're going to retire when you're in your 60s or 70s, you don't pay tax on the money in your IRA until you reach retirement age and begin withdrawing from the account. When you eventually take it out, the money is taxed as ordinary income, which means it's taxed the same way that it would be for wages you've earned subject to federal and state income taxes.

Roth IRA

As with a traditional IRA, you can contribute to a Roth IRA so long as you have earned income and your AGI is below the IRS defined thresholds. The Roth IRA is a favorite of many financial advisors. It's different from the traditional IRA in that it does not give you a tax deduction when you make the contribution. Instead the money you contribute to the account grows tax free. When you reach the retirement age of at least 59 ½ and withdraw from your Roth IRA, based on the laws as they're currently written, you will not pay any taxes on your withdrawal. If that money is $11,000 now and in 25 years it grows to $150,000, you can withdraw it tax free.

For the Roth IRA, there are no age restrictions. If you are retired and end up going back to work and happen to be over 70 ½, you can still contribute to a Roth IRA account.

Simple IRA

A Simple IRA is a company plan that is fairly easy for a business owner to set up for themselves and their employees. The maximum you can contribute is $12,500 a year. The employees and owners contribute using their personal funds up to the yearly maximum of $12,500. There is a catch-up contribution of $3,000, if you are age 50 or over, which brings your maximum contribution to $15,500. Under this plan, the business has to offer a match, which is generally 1% to 3% per year based on each employee's salary.

This is a very simple, easy plan to establish. I work with many people who just want to get a retirement plan started for themselves and their employees, so they choose a Simple IRA initially. After a year or two, they may switch to a different retirement plan which allows larger retirement contributions.

SEP IRA

The SEP IRA has many advantages for business owners. First, it lets you put a lot of money into retirement, and if you do it as a traditional plan, you can save quite a bit of money on your taxes. Another great thing about a SEP IRA is that you can do it in addition to another retirement plan. Let's say that you have a part-time business and you work somewhere else full-time. Your full-time job offers a 401(k) plan and you max that out. Your business can still contribute to a SEP plan.

If you're on payroll for an S corporation that you own, your S corporation can contribute up to 25% of the income on your W-2. If you are an owner/

partner of an LLC or a sole proprietor and do not get a paycheck, your business can contribute 20% of its taxable profits.

The maximum that can be contributed to a SEP IRA is $53,000 in 2017, going up to $54,000 in 2018. If you have already contributed $18,000 to a 401(k), your business could also contribute up to $35,000 to your SEP IRA in 2017. The benefit of doing so lays plainly that if you're able to put away $53,000, which would reduce your taxable income by $53,000 that year, and you could be saving roughly $10,000 plus a year on taxes.

Like the Simple plan, the SEP is a company plan. But unlike the Simple plan, the contributions to the SEP are not made by the employees but rather are contributed by the business. If you have employees and you contribute to the plan yourself as an owner, you also have to make a contribution for your employees. For instance, if you receive a SEP equal to 25% of your payroll, you would then also have to give each of your employees a SEP plan equal to 25% of their pay. There is a way to delay your business having to contribute to your employees SEP plan until they have reached 3 years of employment with your business, and that is by completing a form 5305-SEP.

401(k)

Many people are familiar with a 401(k) from their corporate career. You can contribute more money to this plan than most others. If you're under age 50 (as of 2017), you can contribute $18,000. In 2018, the allowable amount is $18,500. If you're over age 50, you can contribute an additional $6,000—that is $24,000 per year. These funds are contributed by your employees, but if you as the owner want to contribute to your plan, you frequently will need to institute a safe harbor match of approximately 3 ½ % of your employees' salary.

Under the 401(k) plan, as an employer, you are going to have additional costs, fees, and audits associated with your 401(k) plan. You can also set up a profit-sharing or a bonus structure utilizing your 401(k) plan where your business can contribute additional retirement funds above and beyond the $18,000 maximum.

Solo 401(k) with Profit Sharing

For those who qualify, this is my favorite plan for putting away a lot of money for retirement. But in order to contribute to this plan you have to be a one-person business with no employees.

Here is how it works: Let's say you're a sole proprietor and your business makes a net income of $100,000. With this plan, you can first put in the 401(k) maximum, which is $18,000. Then on top of that, you can give yourself profit sharing, which is 20% of that $100,000. So, you could put away $38,000 toward retirement on $100,000 of income. For people who don't have employees and are looking for a way to really max out their retirement plan, this is the plan I would recommend. Like all the other plans, the max on this is $54,000 a year, starting in 2018. Moreover, since this is a 401(k) plan, there are yearly fees that you should inquire about.

Self-Directed IRA

Money in retirement funds is traditionally invested in stocks, bonds, mutual funds, CDs, etc. With Self-Directed IRAs, you have the flexibility to decide to invest in additional channels such as real estate. When you plan this type of investment, note that your retirement fund has to be completely separate from you. If you buy a property using your retirement fund, the purpose should be to rent it out and make income. You cannot use the property personally, nor can you have lateral members of your family occupy it for personal use, because the point is only to produce rental income. Any money that goes out, for instance property repairs, management fees, taxes, is paid through your retirement fund, and any rental income coming in needs to go back into the retirement fund.

There are many intricacies in setting up and properly accounting for your transactions in a Self-Directed IRA so make sure that you obtain advice from competent and qualified CPAs and Self-Directed IRA Custodians.

I have a great deal of experience using Self-Directed IRAs to purchase real estate. In addition to doing it myself for several years, I also work with and teach many individuals on how they can invest in similar ways. I am the CPA spokesperson for Long & Foster Real Estate and have provided training seminars to teams of realtors on this subject.

For more information, visit our video library:
http://www.OsserCPA.com/videos

www.ingramcontent.com/pod-product-compliance
Lightning Source LLC
Chambersburg PA
CBHW052301220526
45471CB00001B/433